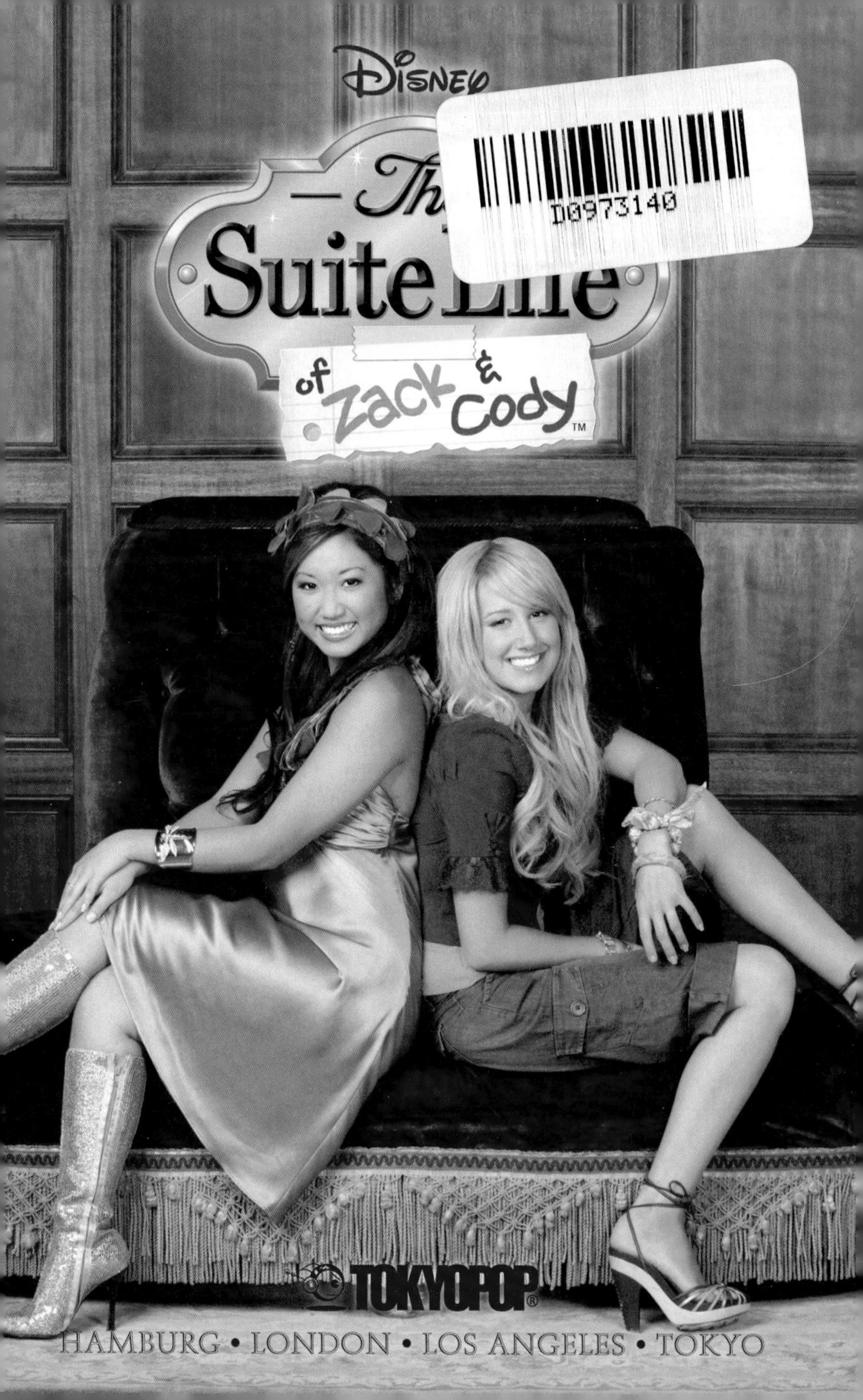
Disney
The Suite Life of Zack & Cody™
TOKYOPOP®
HAMBURG • LONDON • LOS ANGELES • TOKYO

Editor - Julie Taylor
Contributing Editor - Marion Brown
Cover and Graphic Designer - Monalisa J. de Asis
Graphic Artists - Lindsay Seligman and John Lo

Production Manager - Elisabeth Brizzi
Art Director - Anne Marie Horne
VP of Production - Ron Klamert
Editor in Chief - Rob Tokar
Publisher - Mike Kiley
President & C.O.O. - John Parker
C.E.O. & Chief Creative Officer - Stuart Levy

E-mail: info@TOKYOPOP.com
Come visit us online at www.TOKYOPOP.com

A TOKYOPOP® Cine-Manga® Book
TOKYOPOP Inc.
5900 Wilshire Blvd., Suite 2000
Los Angeles, CA 90036

The Suite Life of Zack and Cody
© 2007 Disney

ISBN: 978-1-4278-0703-8

First TOKYOPOP® printing: July 2007

10 9 8 7 6 5 4 3 2

Printed in the USA

Disney

The Suite Life of Zack & Cody™

BASED ON THE TELEVISION SERIES,
"THE SUITE LIFE OF ZACK & CODY,"
CREATED BY DANNY KALLIS & JIM GEOGHAN

CONTENTS:

WHO'S WHO

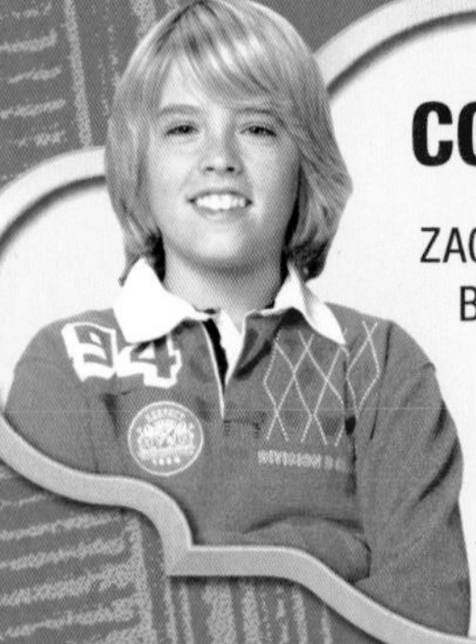

CODY

ZACK'S IMPULSIVE TWIN BROTHER. BOTH HE AND ZACK HAVE A TALENT FOR GETTING IN AND OUT OF TROUBLE.

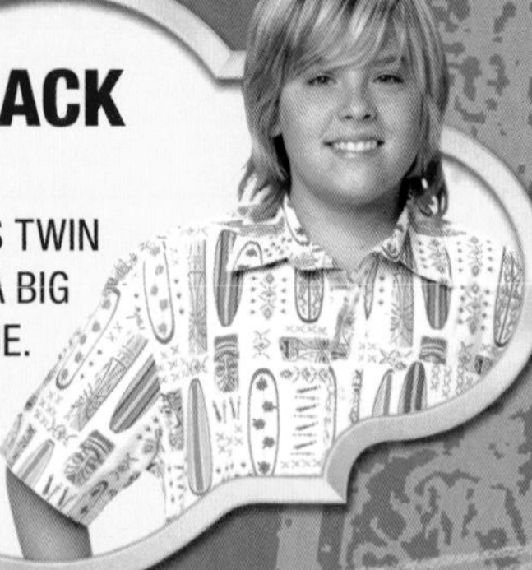

ZACK

CODY'S MISCHEVIOUS TWIN BROTHER. HE HAS A BIG CRUSH ON MADDIE.

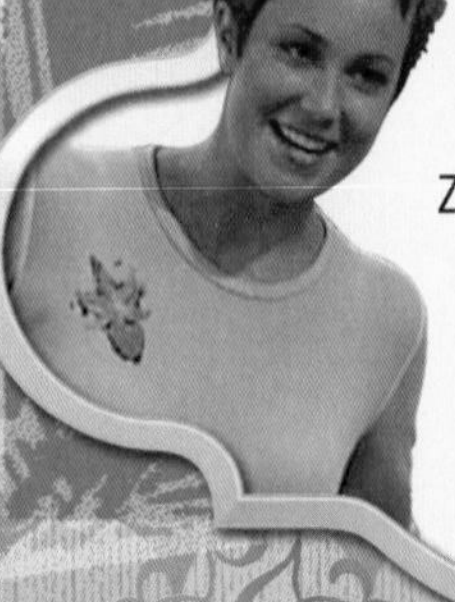

CAREY

ZACK AND CODY'S MOM. SHE IS A SINGER AT THE TIPTON HOTEL, THE SWANKY HOTEL WHERE THEY ALSO LIVE.

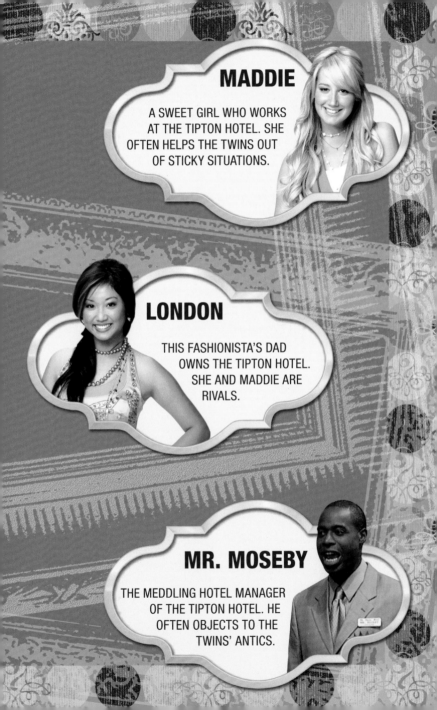

MADDIE

A SWEET GIRL WHO WORKS AT THE TIPTON HOTEL. SHE OFTEN HELPS THE TWINS OUT OF STICKY SITUATIONS.

LONDON

THIS FASHIONISTA'S DAD OWNS THE TIPTON HOTEL. SHE AND MADDIE ARE RIVALS.

MR. MOSEBY

THE MEDDLING HOTEL MANAGER OF THE TIPTON HOTEL. HE OFTEN OBJECTS TO THE TWINS' ANTICS.

Disney

The Suite Life of Zack & Cody

HOTEL HANGOUT

BASED ON THE EPISODE
WRITTEN BY JENY QUINE

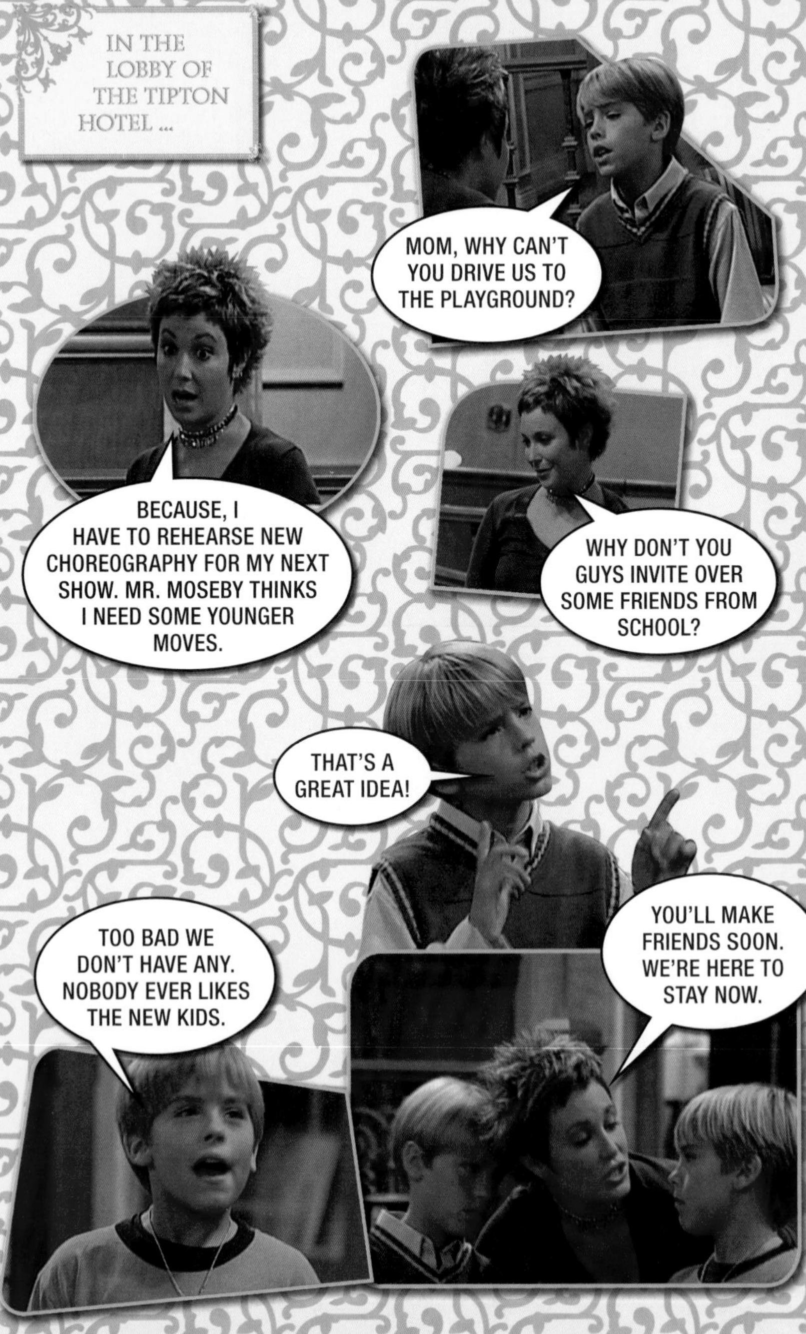
IN THE LOBBY OF THE TIPTON HOTEL ...
MOM, WHY CAN'T YOU DRIVE US TO THE PLAYGROUND?
BECAUSE, I HAVE TO REHEARSE NEW CHOREOGRAPHY FOR MY NEXT SHOW. MR. MOSEBY THINKS I NEED SOME YOUNGER MOVES.
WHY DON'T YOU GUYS INVITE OVER SOME FRIENDS FROM SCHOOL?
THAT'S A GREAT IDEA!
TOO BAD WE DON'T HAVE ANY. NOBODY EVER LIKES THE NEW KIDS.
YOU'LL MAKE FRIENDS SOON. WE'RE HERE TO STAY NOW.

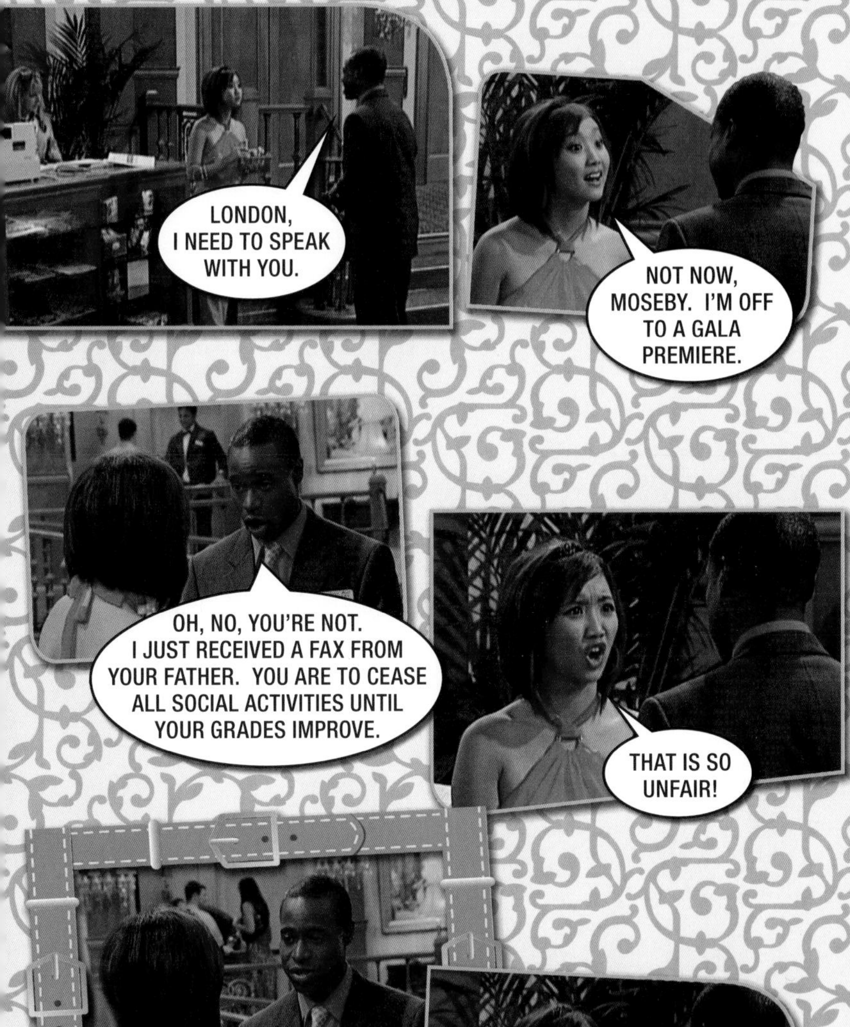
LONDON, I NEED TO SPEAK WITH YOU.
NOT NOW, MOSEBY. I'M OFF TO A GALA PREMIERE.
OH, NO, YOU'RE NOT. I JUST RECEIVED A FAX FROM YOUR FATHER. YOU ARE TO CEASE ALL SOCIAL ACTIVITIES UNTIL YOUR GRADES IMPROVE.
THAT IS SO UNFAIR!
HE ALSO INSISTED I HIRE YOU A TUTOR.
WHEN IS HE GOING TO REALIZE THAT EDUCATION AND ME JUST DON'T MIX?

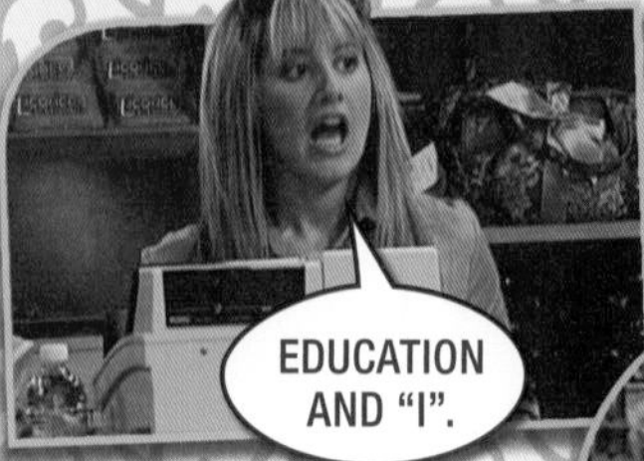
EDUCATION AND "I".

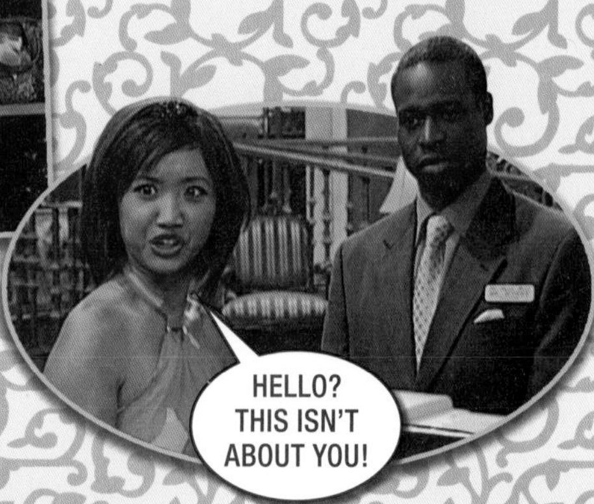
HELLO? THIS ISN'T ABOUT YOU!

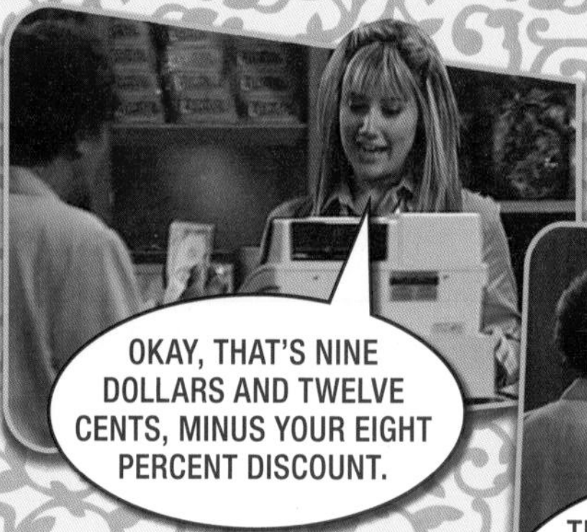
OKAY, THAT'S NINE DOLLARS AND TWELVE CENTS, MINUS YOUR EIGHT PERCENT DISCOUNT.

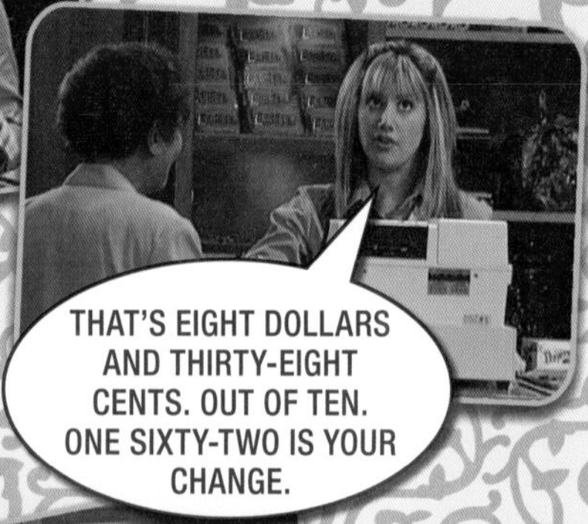
THAT'S EIGHT DOLLARS AND THIRTY-EIGHT CENTS. OUT OF TEN. ONE SIXTY-TWO IS YOUR CHANGE.

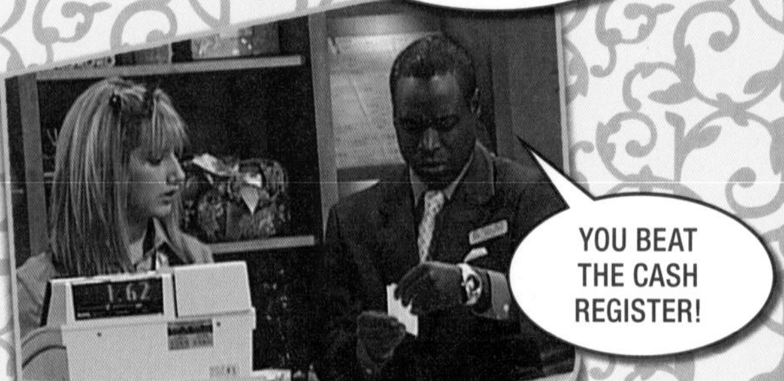
YOU BEAT THE CASH REGISTER!

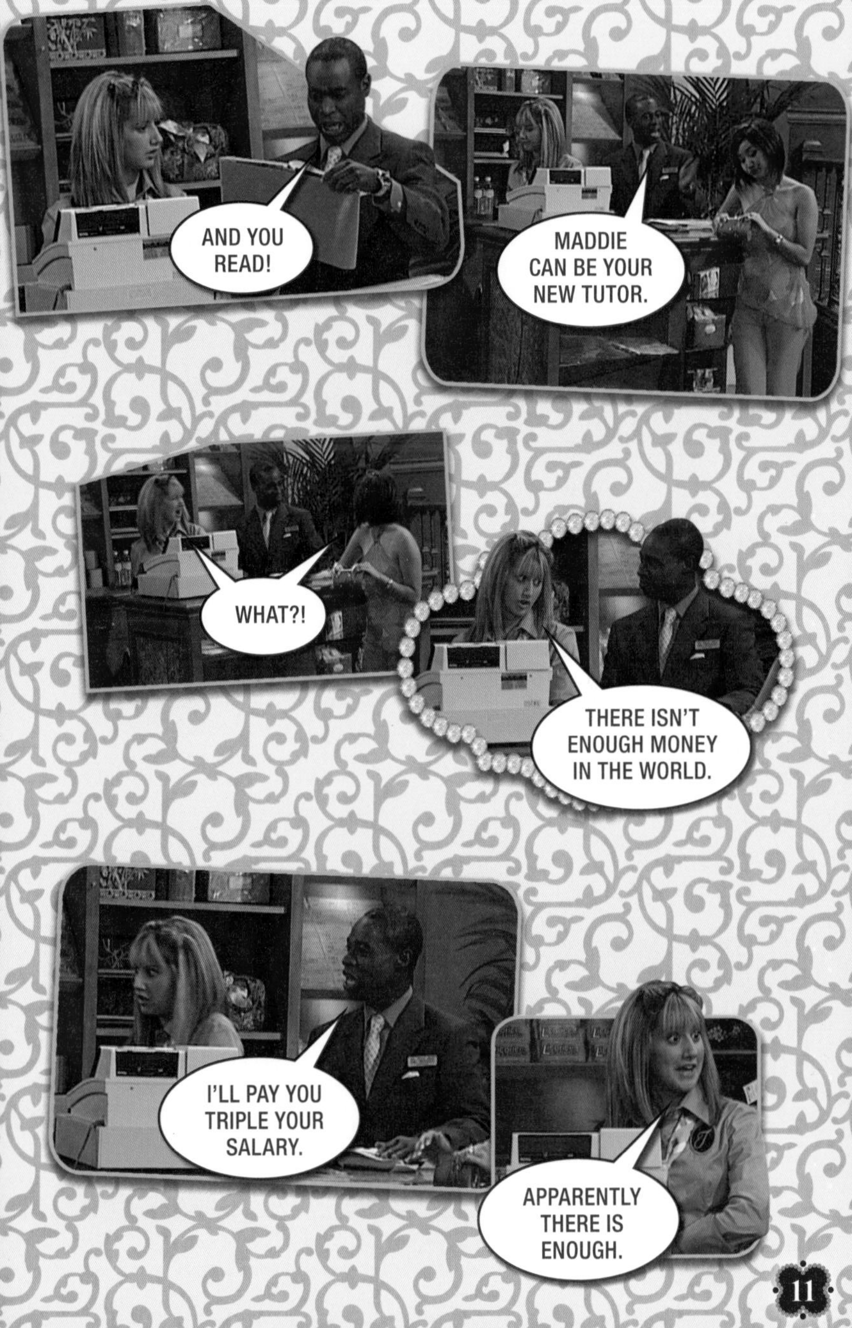
AND YOU READ!
MADDIE CAN BE YOUR NEW TUTOR.
WHAT?!
THERE ISN'T ENOUGH MONEY IN THE WORLD.
I'LL PAY YOU TRIPLE YOUR SALARY.
APPARENTLY THERE IS ENOUGH.

IN THE SCHOOLYARD...

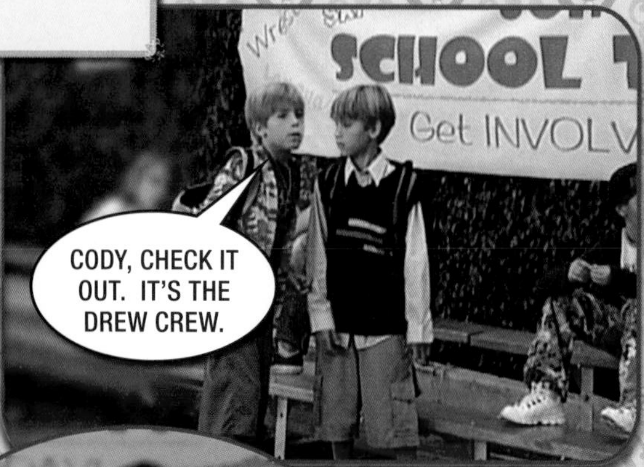
SCHOOL
Get INVOLV
CODY, CHECK IT OUT. IT'S THE DREW CREW.

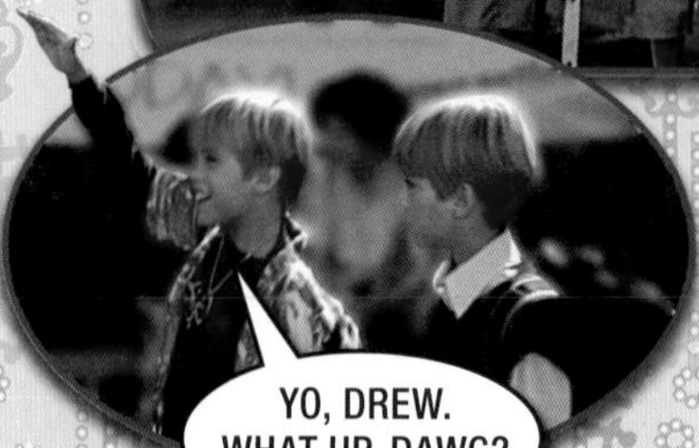
YO, DREW. WHAT UP, DAWG?

DREW CALLS THE TWINS "THE CLONES."

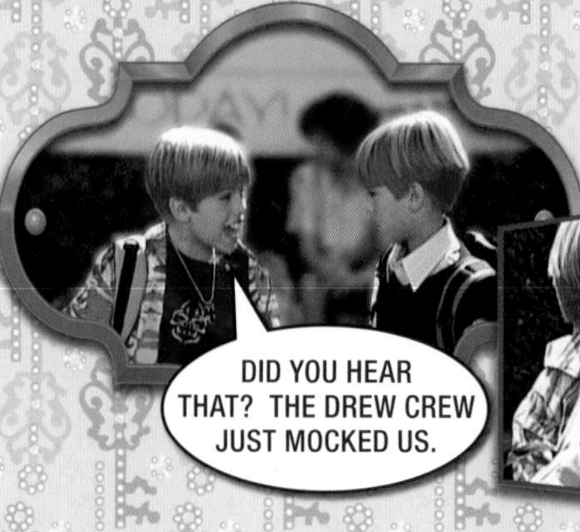
DID YOU HEAR THAT? THE DREW CREW JUST MOCKED US.

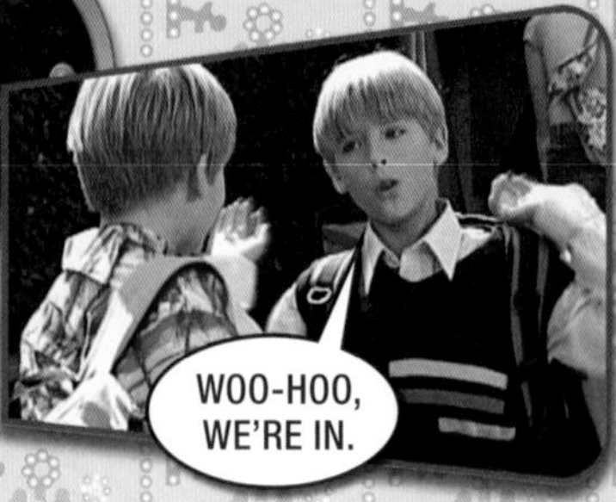
WOO-HOO, WE'RE IN.

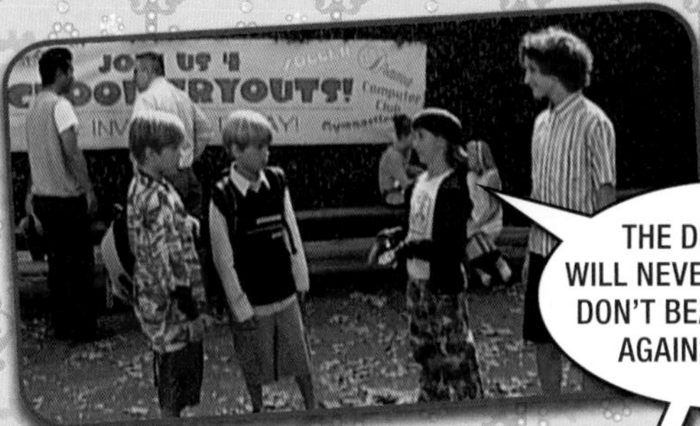
THE DREW CREW WILL NEVER ACCEPT YOU. DON'T BEAT YOUR HEAD AGAINST A WALL.
I'M MAX, BY THE WAY. AND THIS IS TAPEWORM.

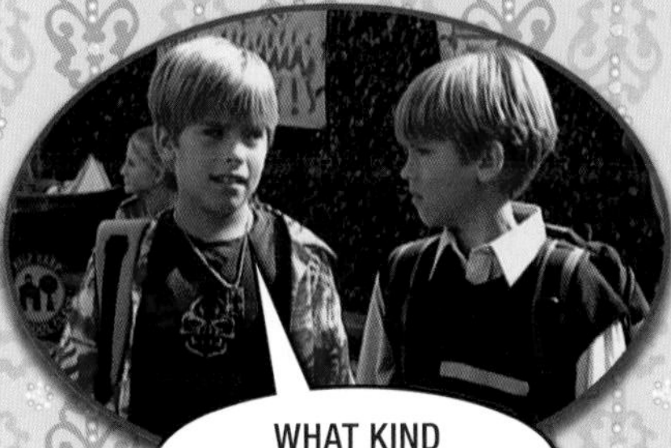
WHAT KIND OF NAME IS THAT?

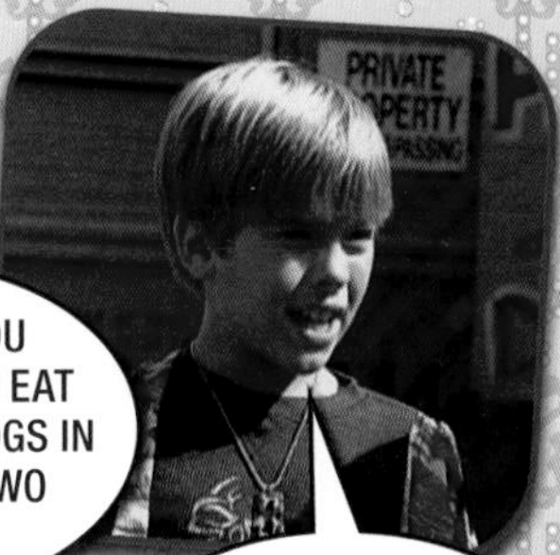
THE KIND YOU GET WHEN YOU EAT TWENTY HOT DOGS IN LESS THAN TWO MINUTES.
COOL, BEATS MY RECORD.

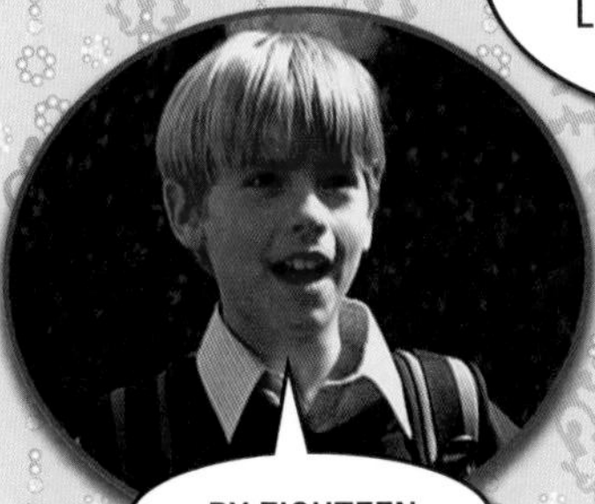
BY EIGHTEEN.

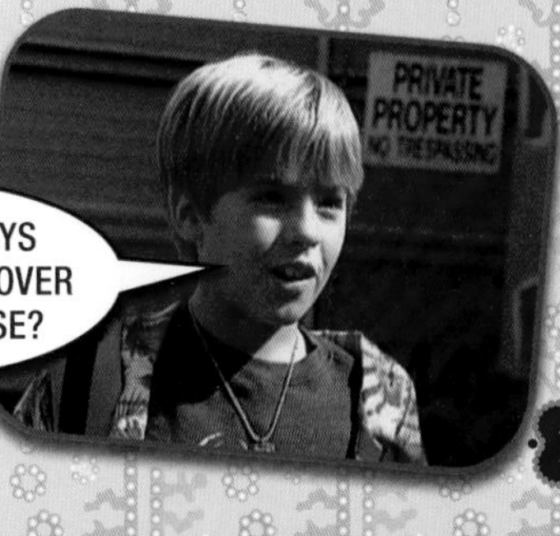
PRIVATE PROPERTY
NO TRESPASSING
HEY, YOU GUYS WANNA COME OVER TO OUR HOUSE?

BACK AT THE HOTEL...

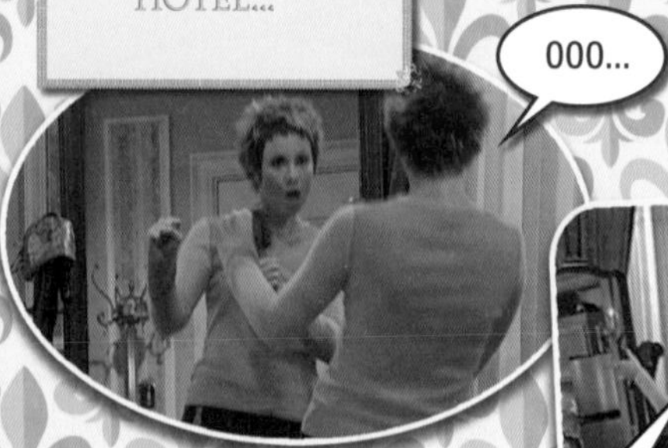
OOO...

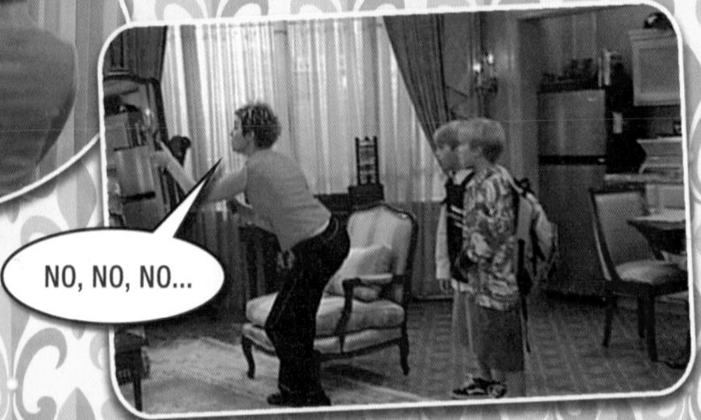
NO, NO, NO...

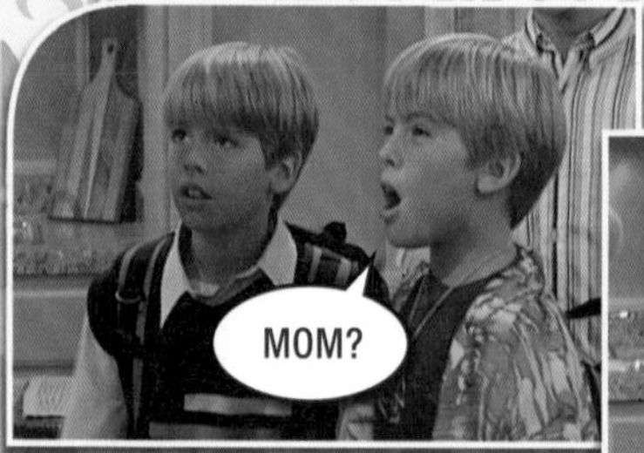
MOM?

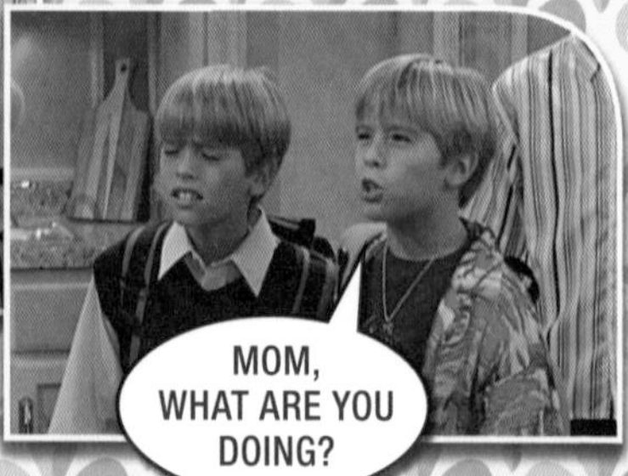
MOM, WHAT ARE YOU DOING?

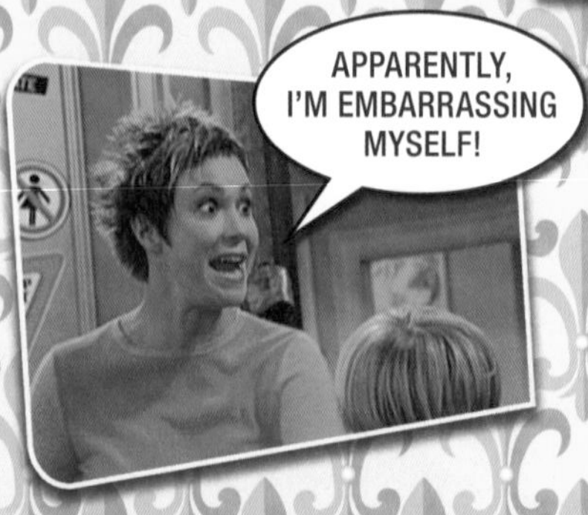
APPARENTLY, I'M EMBARRASSING MYSELF!

THE TWINS INTRODUCE THEIR MOM TO MAX AND TAPEWORM, AND MAX SHOWS CAREY SOME DANCE MOVES.

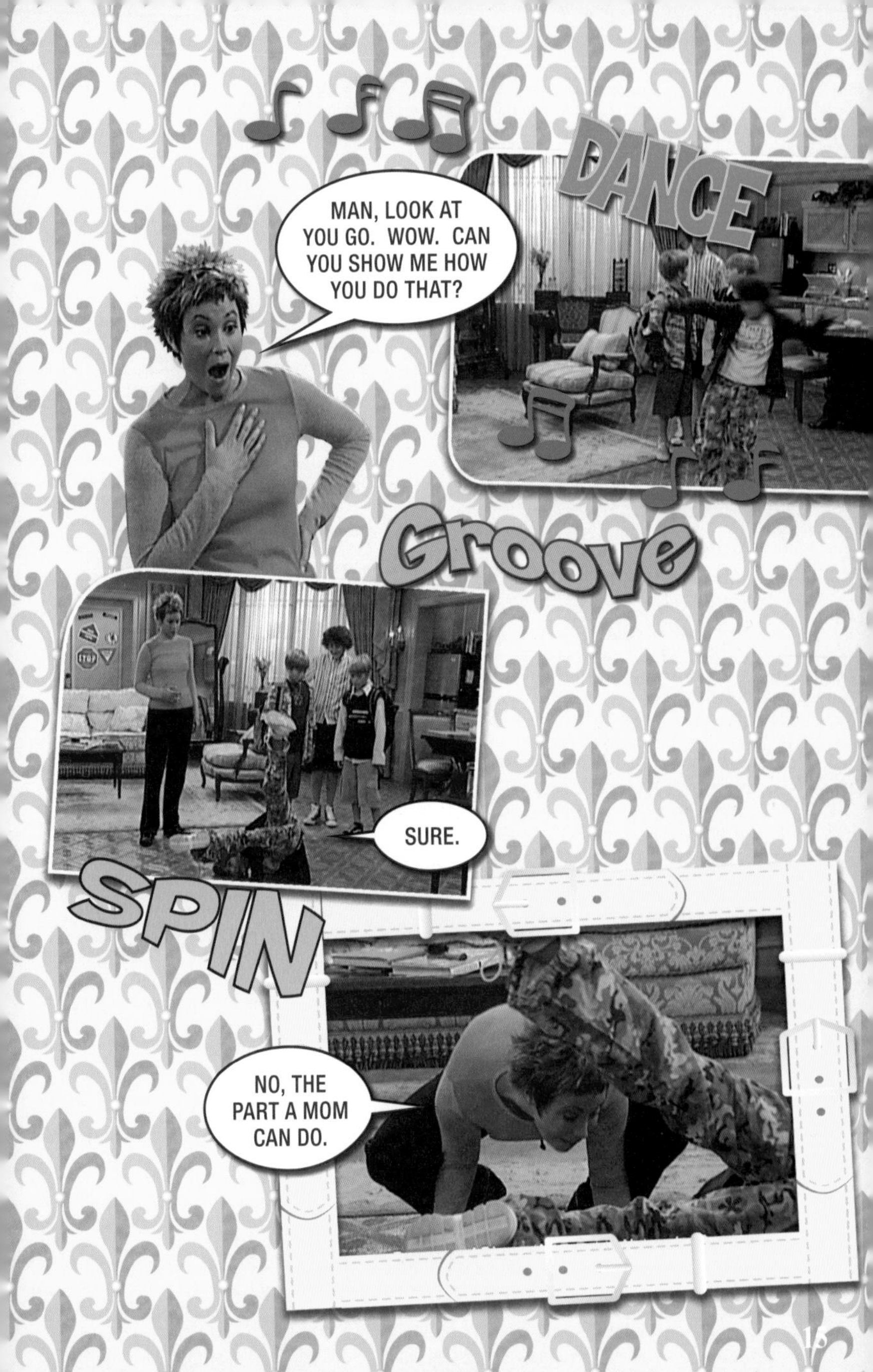
DANCE
MAN, LOOK AT YOU GO. WOW. CAN YOU SHOW ME HOW YOU DO THAT?
Groove
SURE.
SPIN
NO, THE PART A MOM CAN DO.

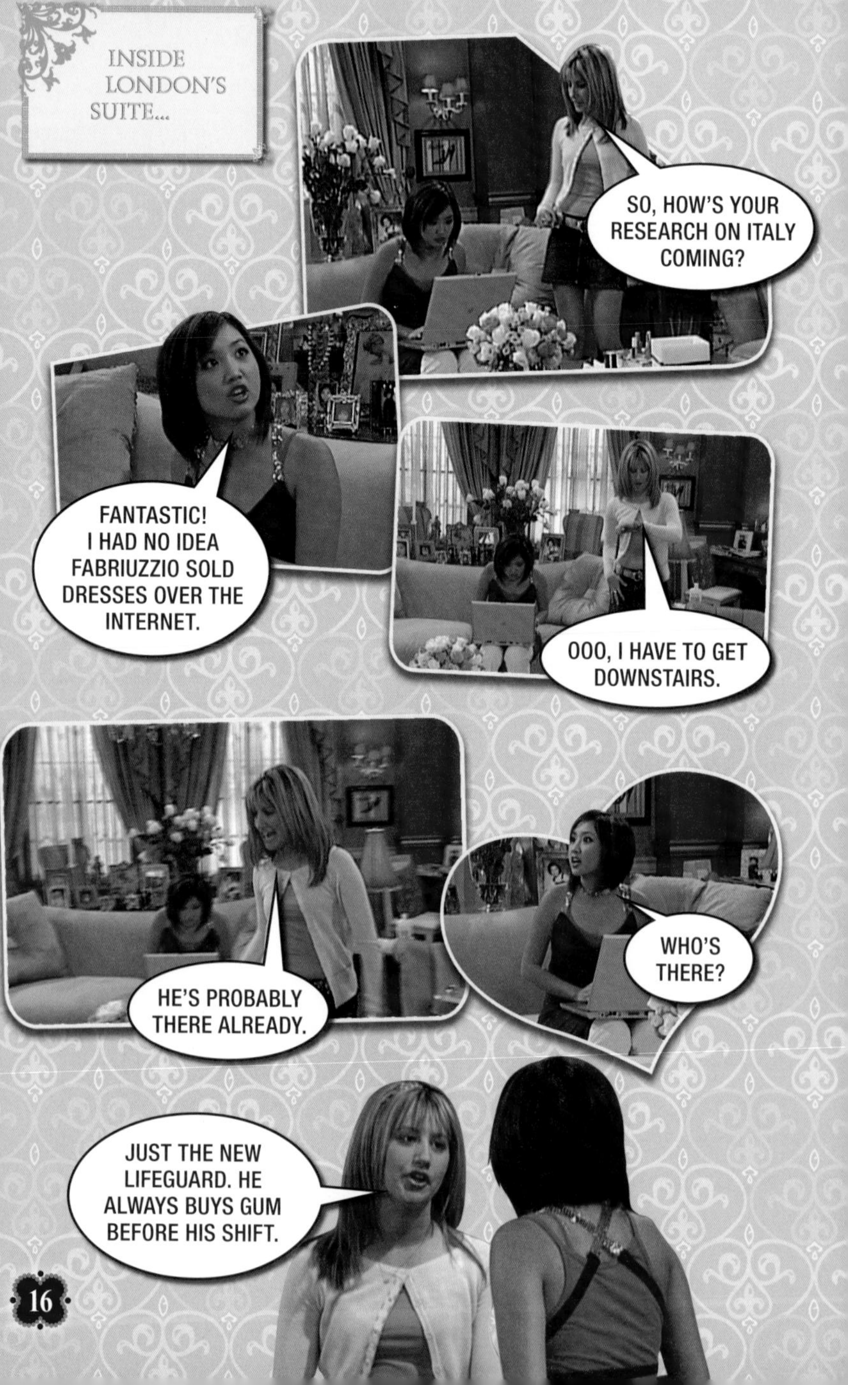
INSIDE LONDON'S SUITE...
SO, HOW'S YOUR RESEARCH ON ITALY COMING?
FANTASTIC! I HAD NO IDEA FABRIUZZIO SOLD DRESSES OVER THE INTERNET.
OOO, I HAVE TO GET DOWNSTAIRS.
HE'S PROBABLY THERE ALREADY.
WHO'S THERE?
JUST THE NEW LIFEGUARD. HE ALWAYS BUYS GUM BEFORE HIS SHIFT.

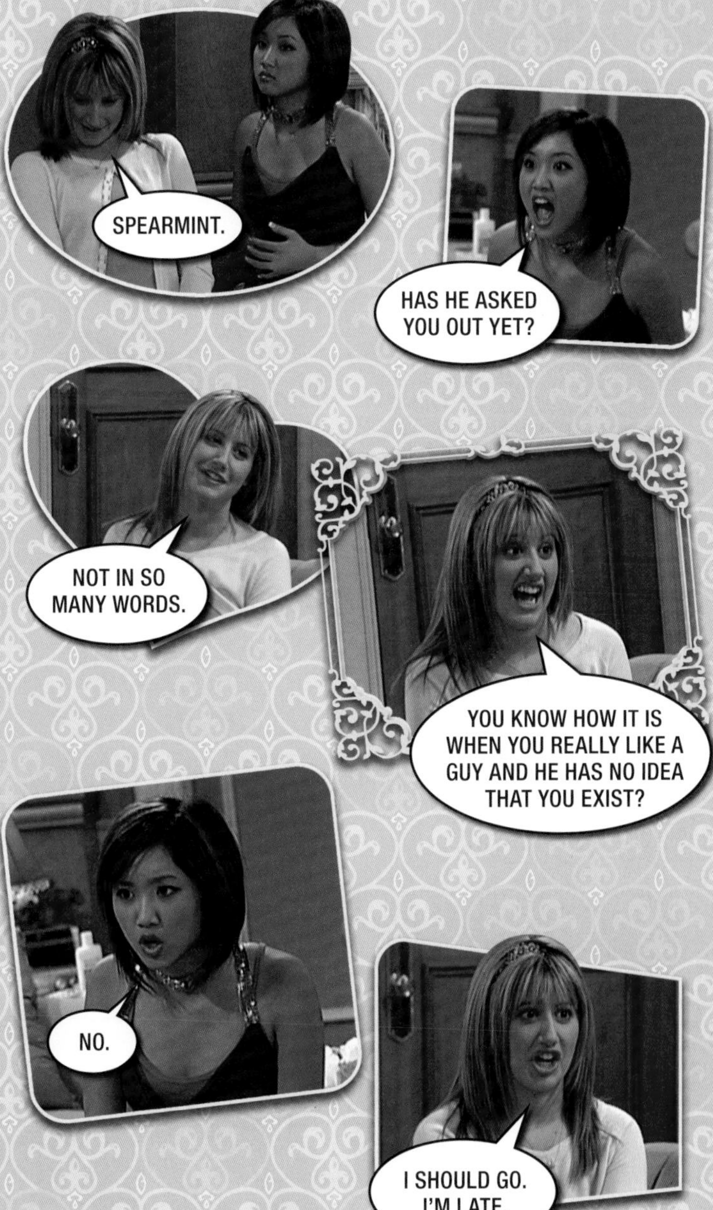
SPEARMINT.
HAS HE ASKED YOU OUT YET?
NOT IN SO MANY WORDS.
YOU KNOW HOW IT IS WHEN YOU REALLY LIKE A GUY AND HE HAS NO IDEA THAT YOU EXIST?
NO.
I SHOULD GO. I'M LATE.

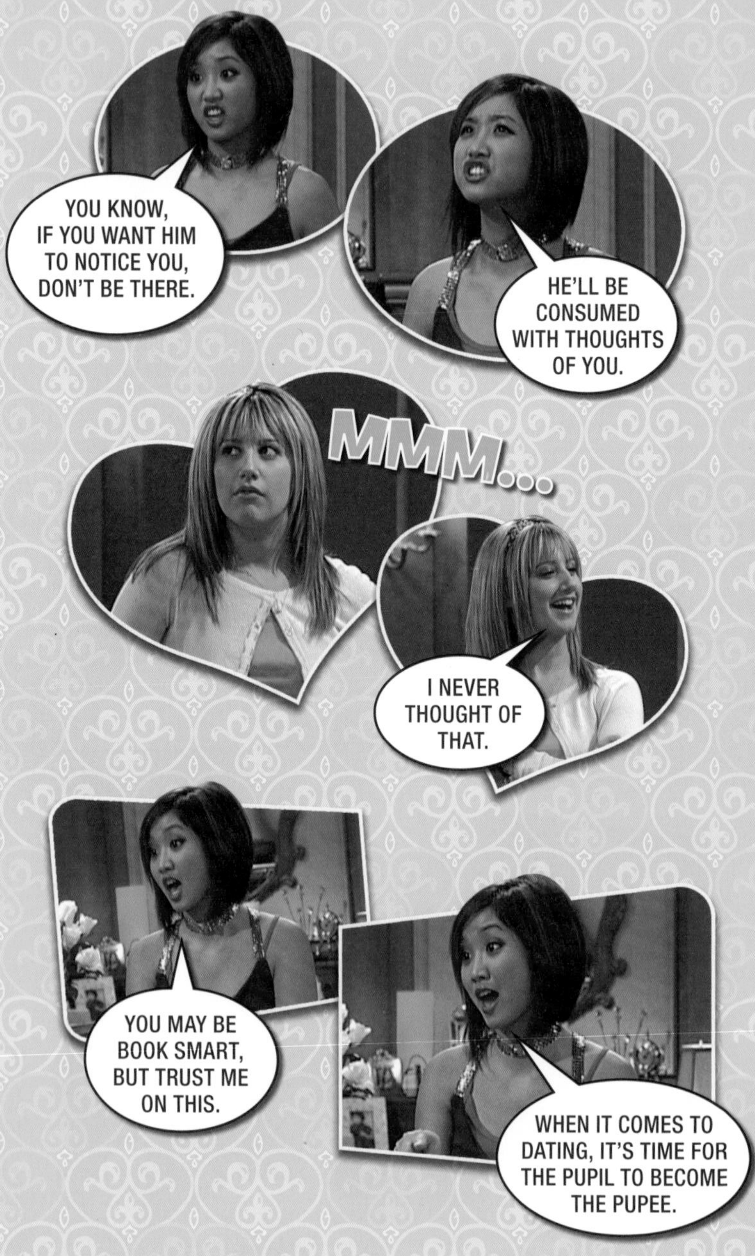
YOU KNOW, IF YOU WANT HIM TO NOTICE YOU, DON'T BE THERE.
HE'LL BE CONSUMED WITH THOUGHTS OF YOU.
MMM...
I NEVER THOUGHT OF THAT.
YOU MAY BE BOOK SMART, BUT TRUST ME ON THIS.
WHEN IT COMES TO DATING, IT'S TIME FOR THE PUPIL TO BECOME THE PUPEE.

MEANWHILE BACK IN SCHOOL...

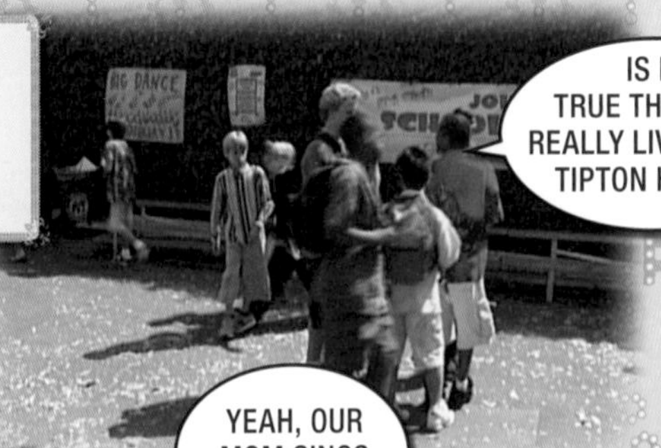
IS IT TRUE THAT YOU REALLY LIVE IN THE TIPTON HOTEL?

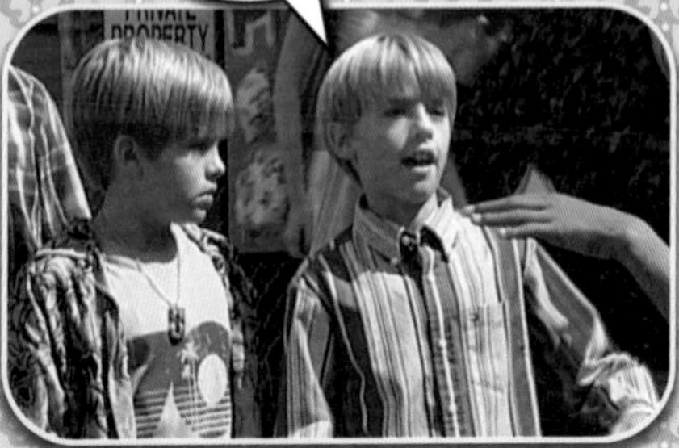
YEAH, OUR MOM SINGS THERE.

DREW ASKS IF THERE ARE REALLY HOT BABES SERVING ICE CREAM BY THE POOL.

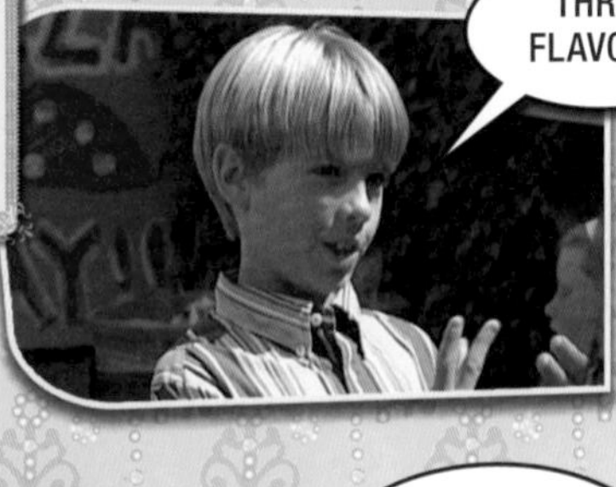
THREE FLAVORS.

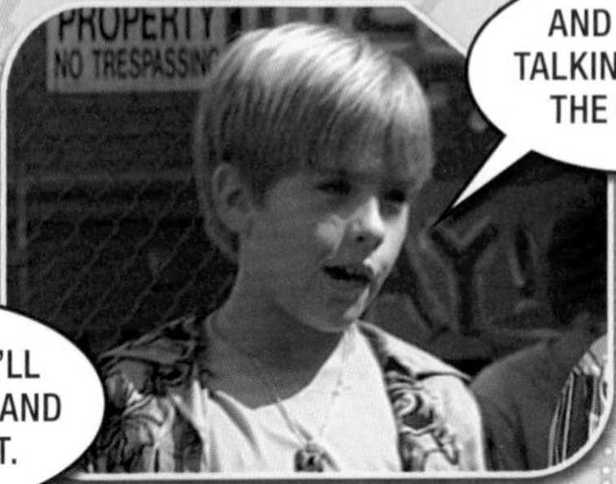
PROPERTY
AND WE'RE TALKING ABOUT THE GIRLS.
MAYBE WE'LL COME OVER AND HANG OUT.

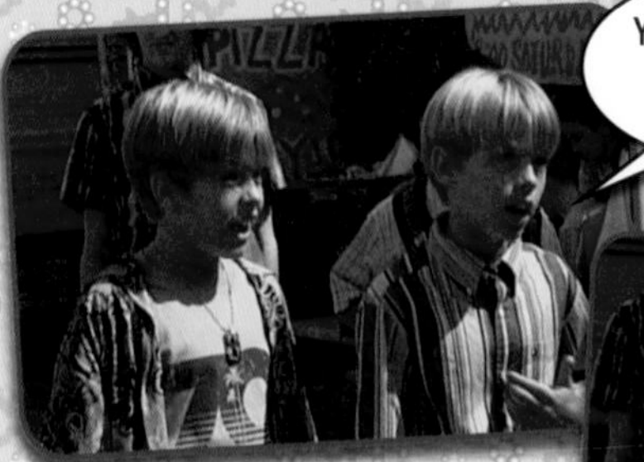
YOU WANT TO HANG OUT WITH US?

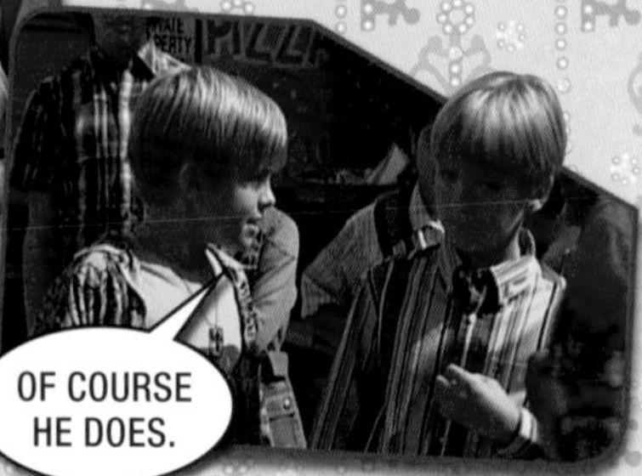
OF COURSE HE DOES.

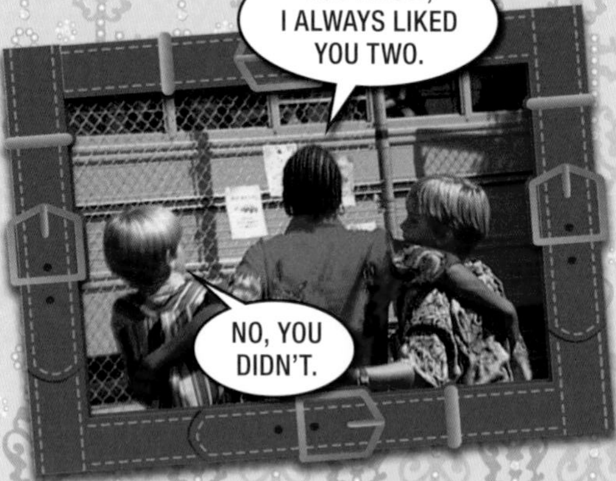
YOU KNOW, I ALWAYS LIKED YOU TWO.
NO, YOU DIDN'T.

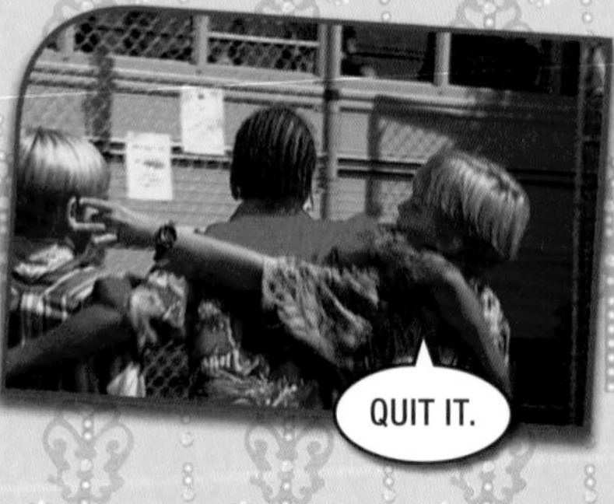
QUIT IT.

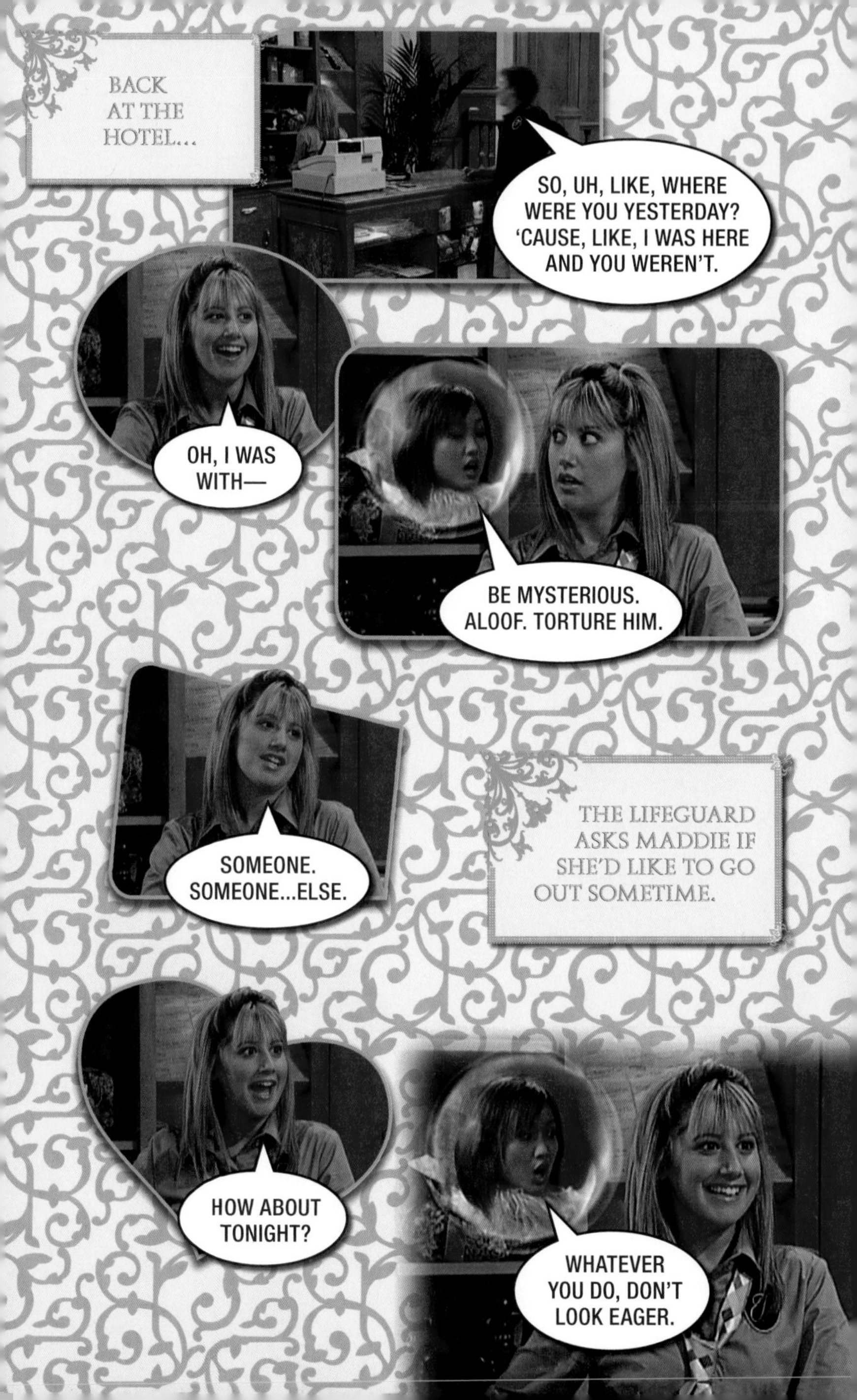
BACK AT THE HOTEL...
SO, UH, LIKE, WHERE WERE YOU YESTERDAY? 'CAUSE, LIKE, I WAS HERE AND YOU WEREN'T.
OH, I WAS WITH—
BE MYSTERIOUS. ALOOF. TORTURE HIM.
SOMEONE. SOMEONE...ELSE.
THE LIFEGUARD ASKS MADDIE IF SHE'D LIKE TO GO OUT SOMETIME.
HOW ABOUT TONIGHT?
WHATEVER YOU DO, DON'T LOOK EAGER.

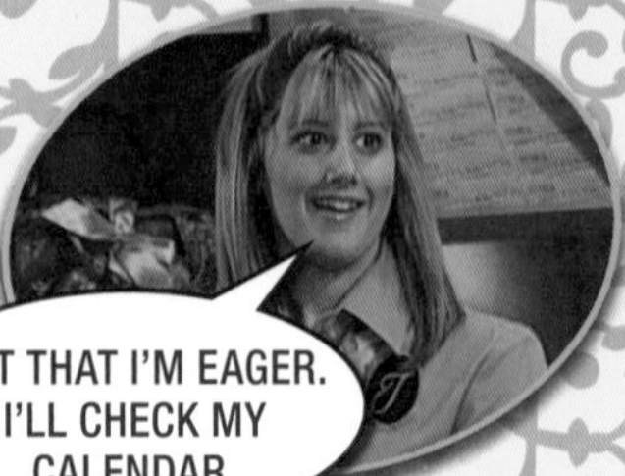
NOT THAT I'M EAGER. I'LL CHECK MY CALENDAR.

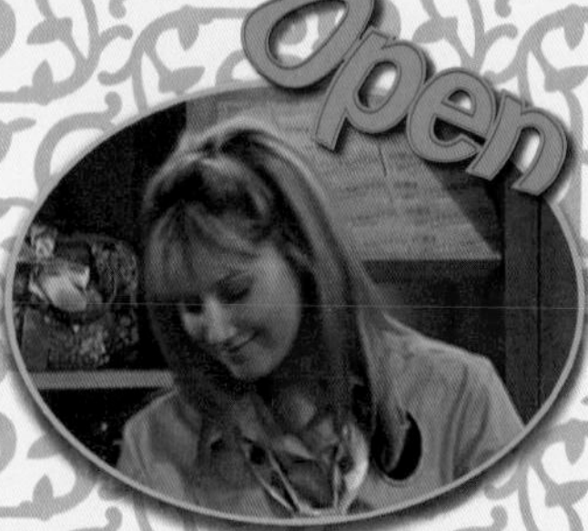
Open

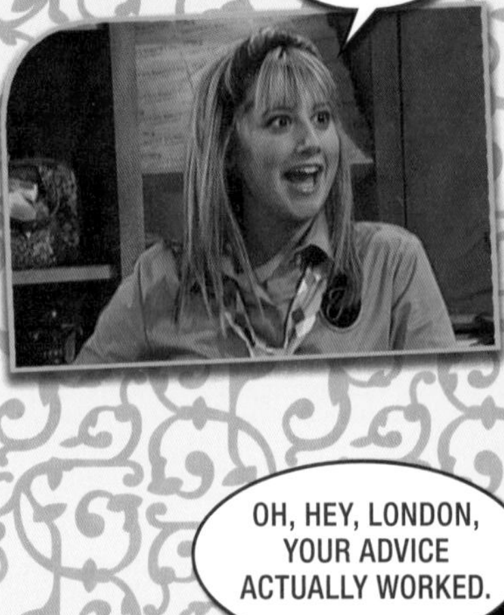
I'M FREE.

THEY MAKE PLANS TO HAVE DINNER AT THE SEAPORT, THEN LANCE THE LIFEGUARD DEPARTS.

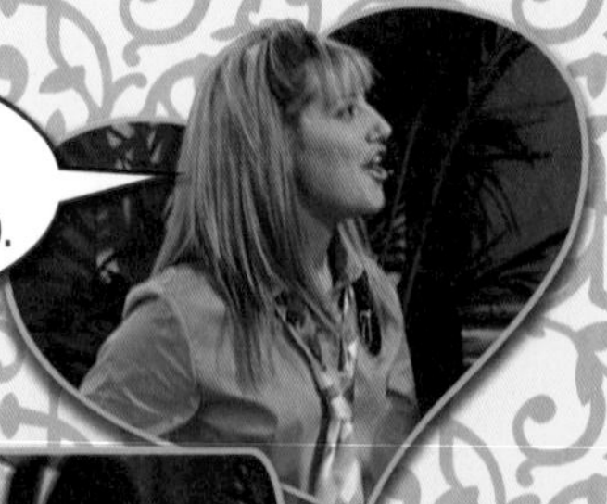
OH, HEY, LONDON, YOUR ADVICE ACTUALLY WORKED.

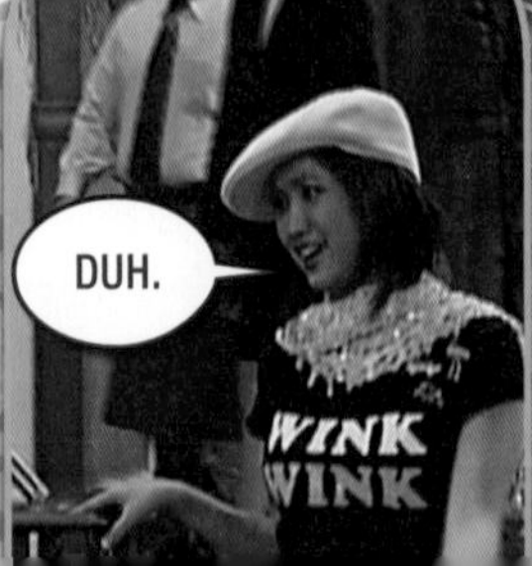
DUH.
WINK
WINK

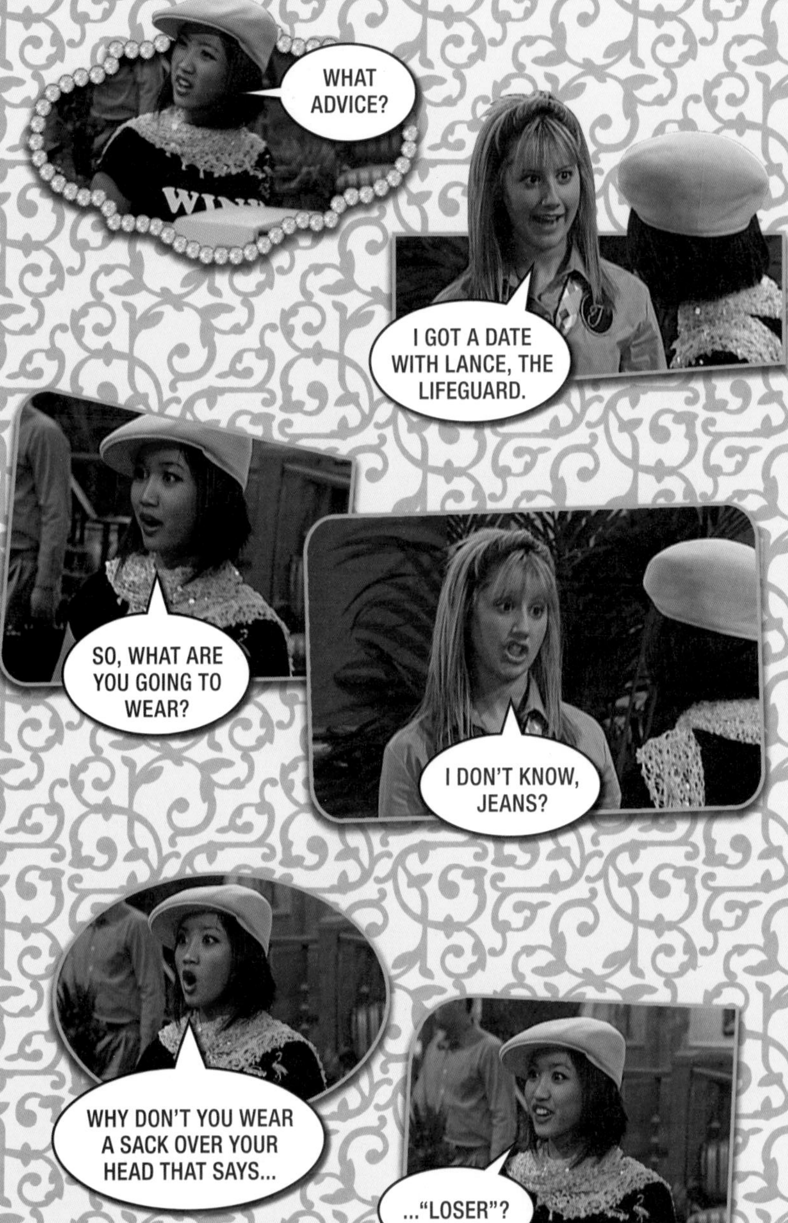
WHAT ADVICE?
I GOT A DATE WITH LANCE, THE LIFEGUARD.
SO, WHAT ARE YOU GOING TO WEAR?
I DON'T KNOW, JEANS?
WHY DON'T YOU WEAR A SACK OVER YOUR HEAD THAT SAYS...
..."LOSER"?

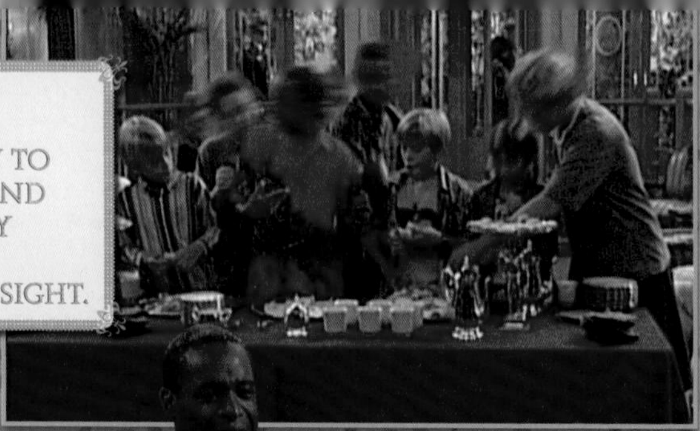
THE TWINS BRING THE DREW CREW TO THE HOTEL...AND THEY INSTANTLY START EATING EVERYTHING IN SIGHT.

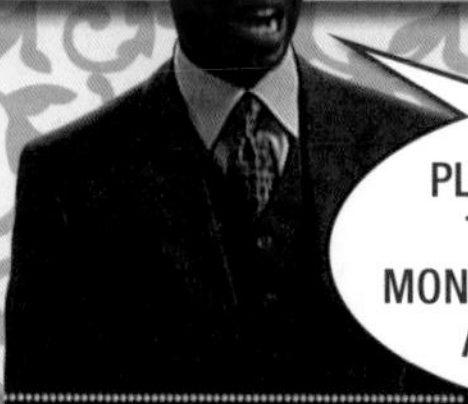
PLEASE TAKE HIM AND THE REST OF YOUR MONGREL HORDE UPSTAIRS AND OUT OF SIGHT.

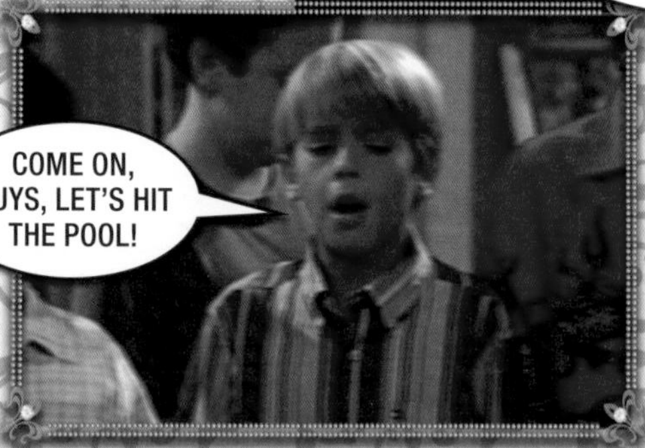
COME ON, GUYS, LET'S HIT THE POOL!

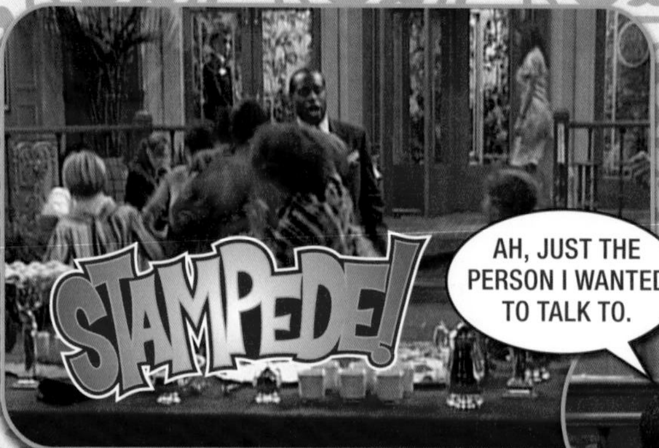
STAMPEDE!

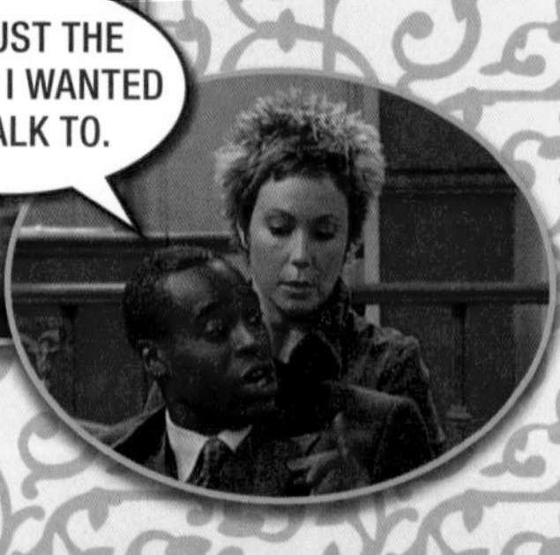
AH, JUST THE PERSON I WANTED TO TALK TO.

AT THE ROOFTOP POOL...

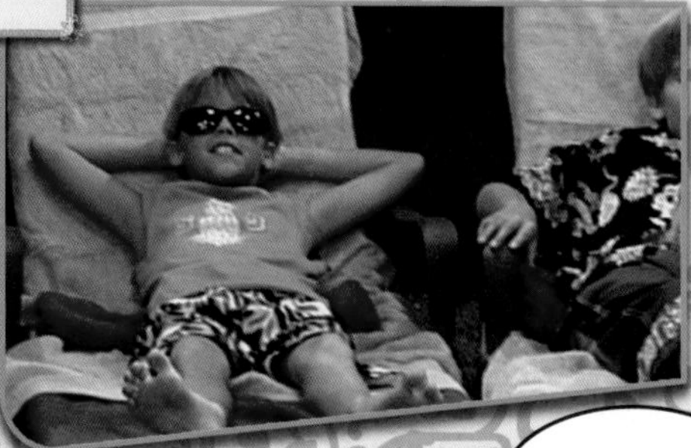

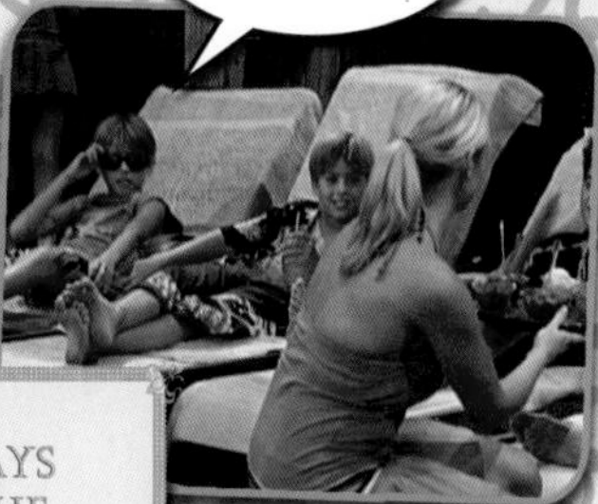
FOUR O'CLOCK ICE CREAM.

DREW SAYS MAYBE THE TWINS AREN'T SO LAME AFTER ALL.

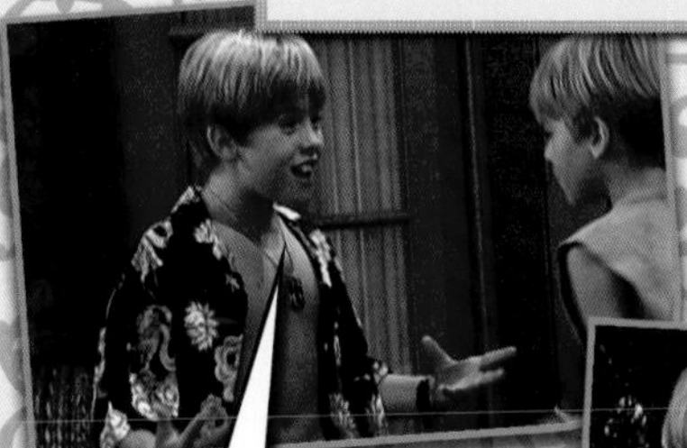
DID YOU HEAR THAT? WE'RE IN! WE'RE NOT SO LAME.

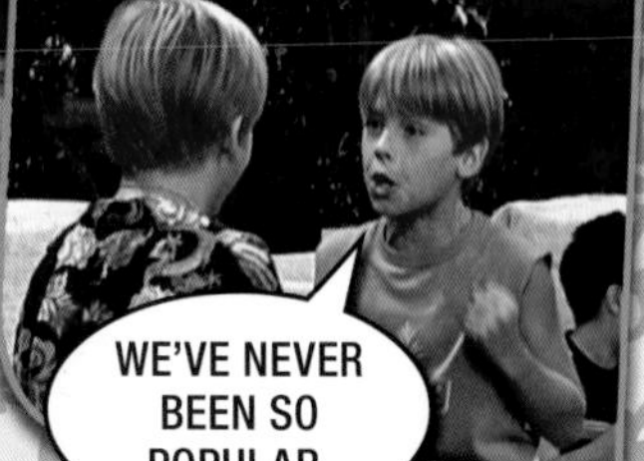
WE'VE NEVER BEEN SO POPULAR.

THE DREW CREW IS RUDE TO MAX AND TAPEWORM... AND DREW SOON SAYS, "HEY, YA'LL, LET'S DITCH THE DWEEBS."

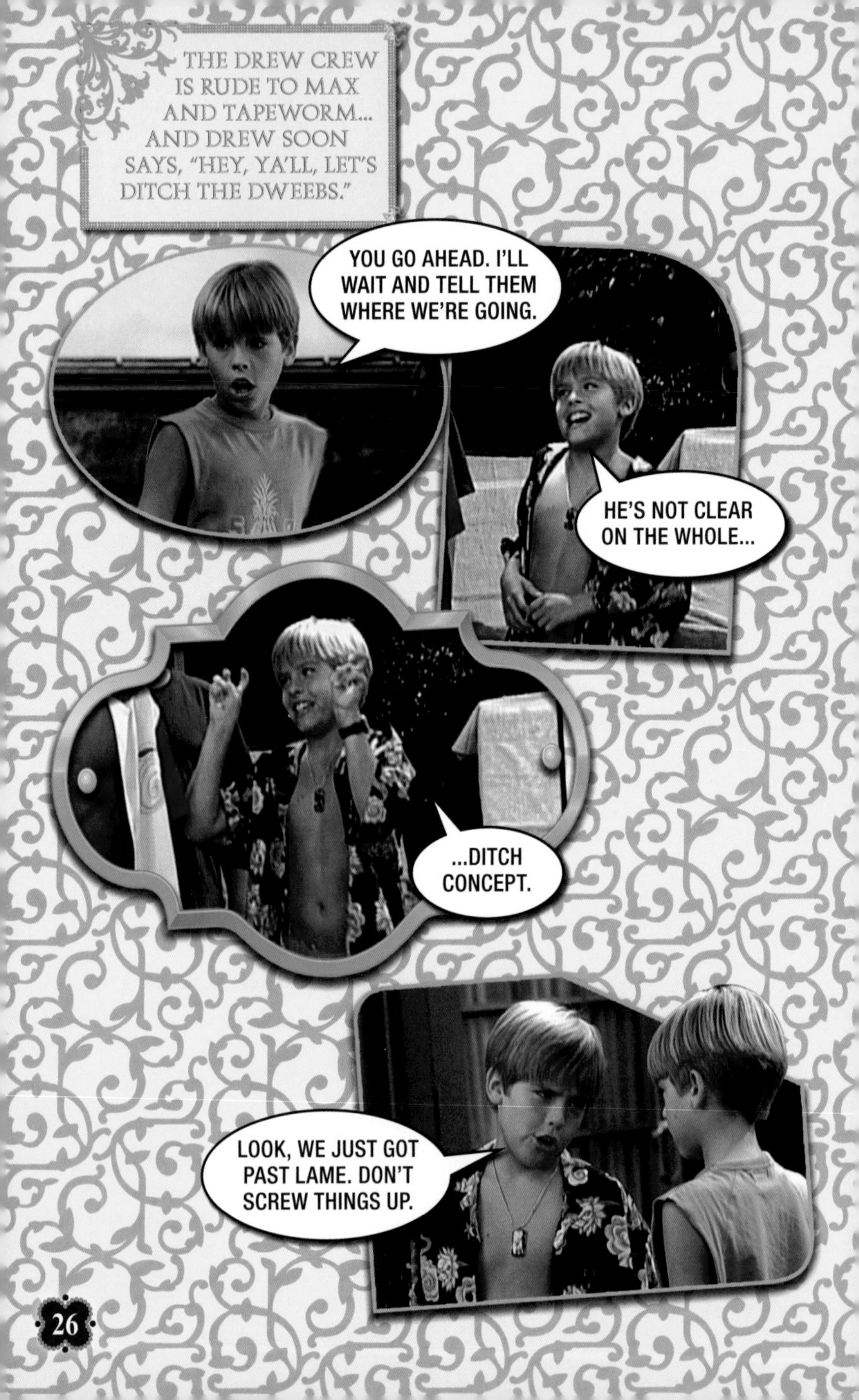
YOU GO AHEAD. I'LL WAIT AND TELL THEM WHERE WE'RE GOING.
HE'S NOT CLEAR ON THE WHOLE...
...DITCH CONCEPT.
LOOK, WE JUST GOT PAST LAME. DON'T SCREW THINGS UP.

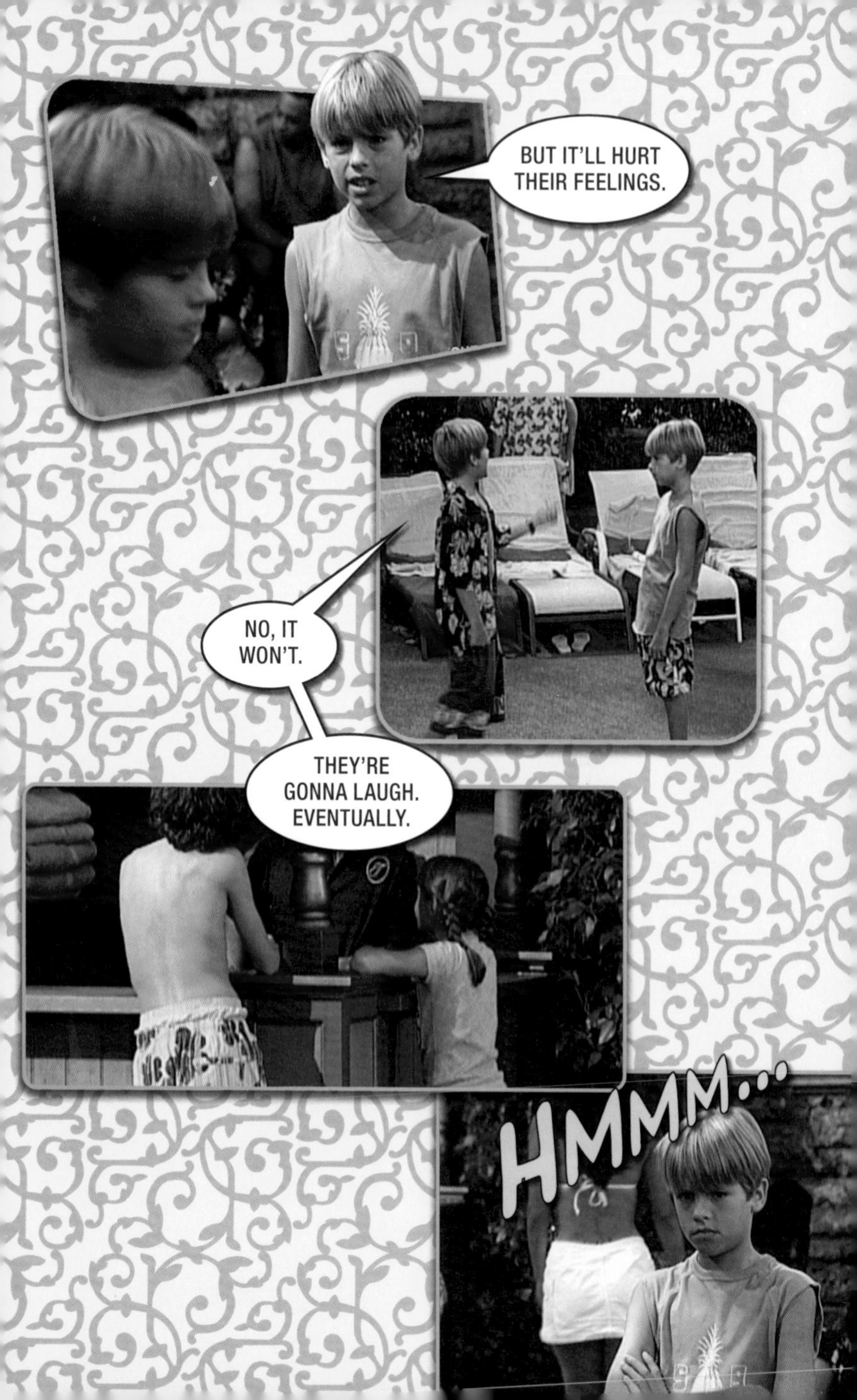
BUT IT'LL HURT THEIR FEELINGS.
NO, IT WON'T.
THEY'RE GONNA LAUGH. EVENTUALLY.
HMMM...

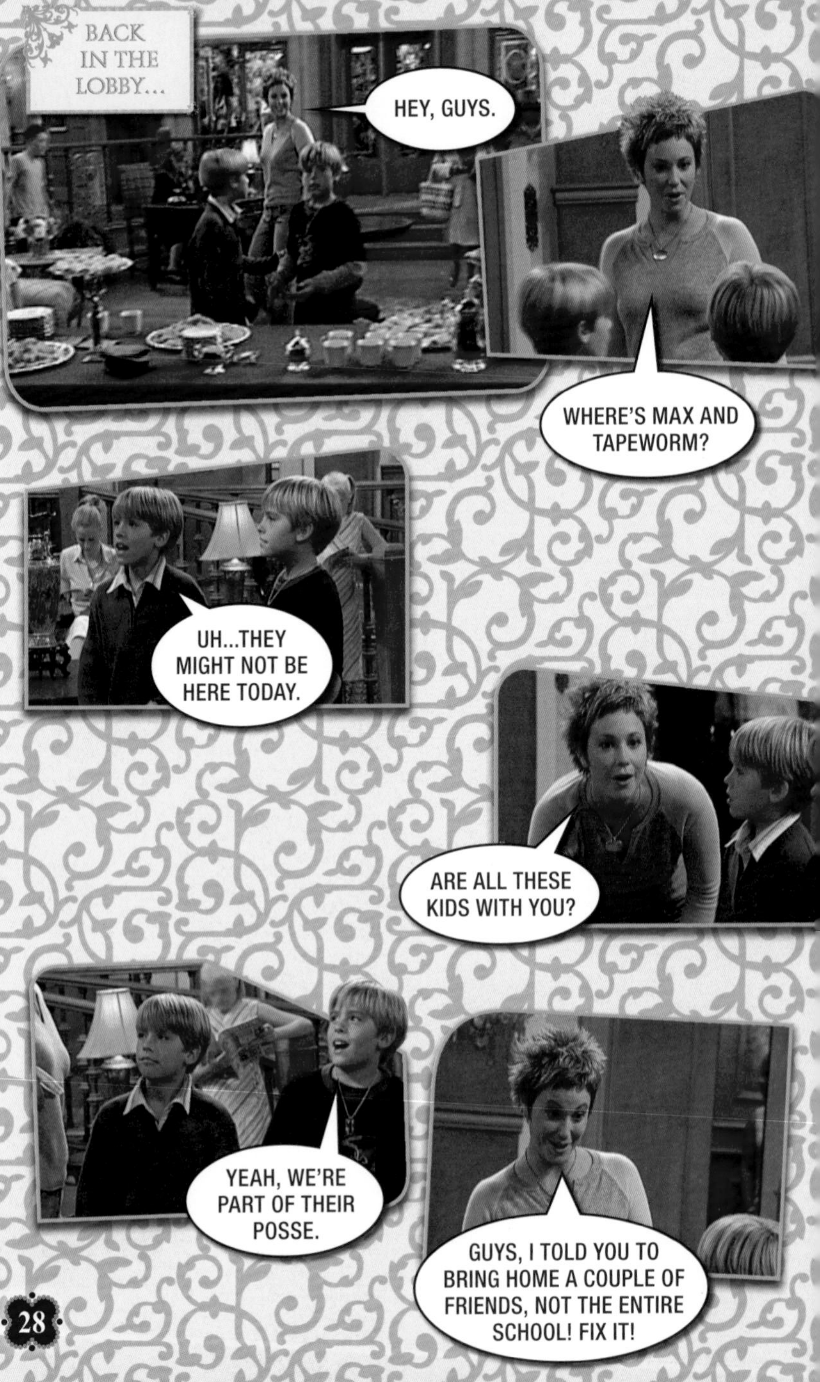
BACK IN THE LOBBY...
HEY, GUYS.
WHERE'S MAX AND TAPEWORM?
UH...THEY MIGHT NOT BE HERE TODAY.
ARE ALL THESE KIDS WITH YOU?
YEAH, WE'RE PART OF THEIR POSSE.
GUYS, I TOLD YOU TO BRING HOME A COUPLE OF FRIENDS, NOT THE ENTIRE SCHOOL! FIX IT!

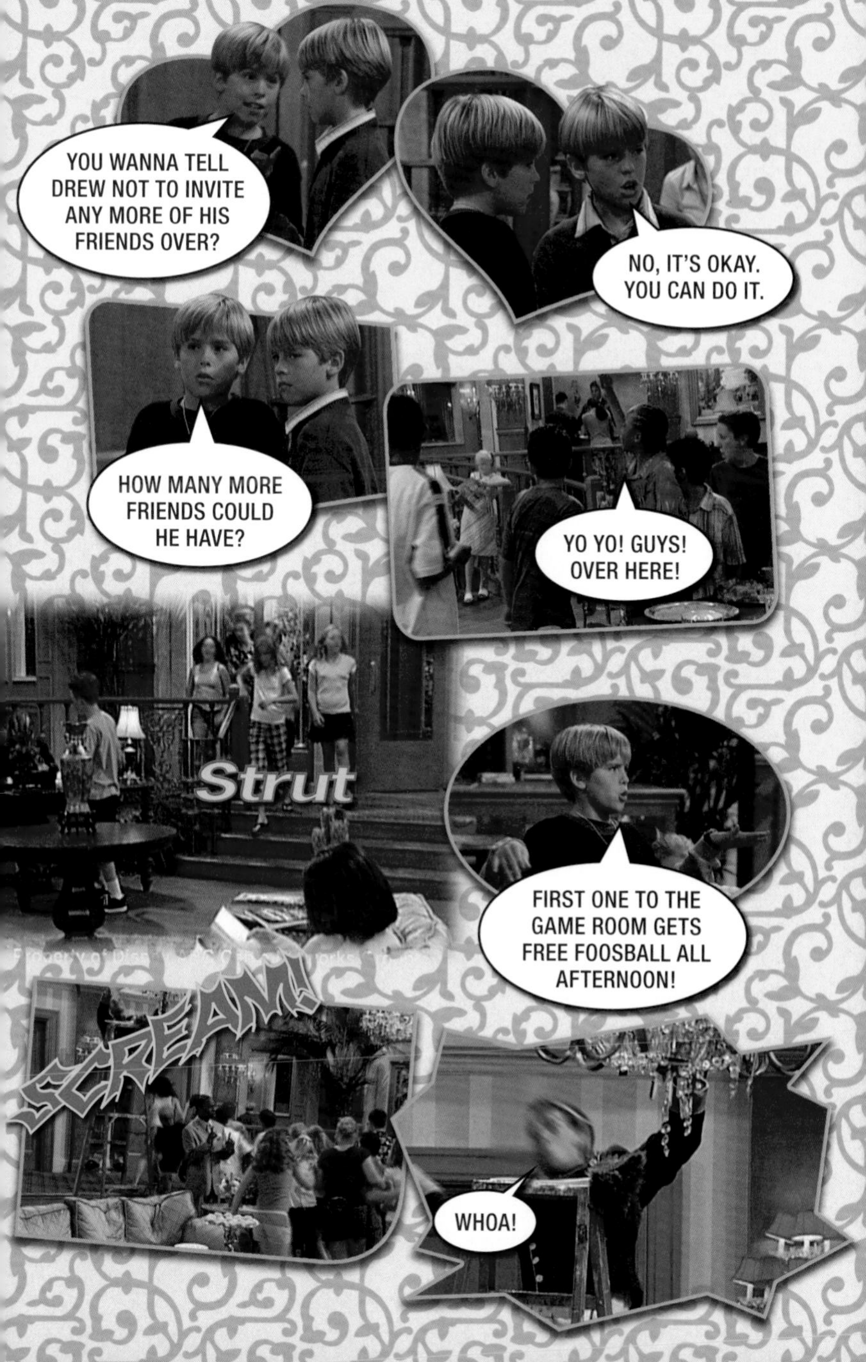
YOU WANNA TELL DREW NOT TO INVITE ANY MORE OF HIS FRIENDS OVER?
NO, IT'S OKAY. YOU CAN DO IT.
HOW MANY MORE FRIENDS COULD HE HAVE?
YO YO! GUYS! OVER HERE!
Strut
FIRST ONE TO THE GAME ROOM GETS FREE FOOSBALL ALL AFTERNOON!
SCREAM!
WHOA!

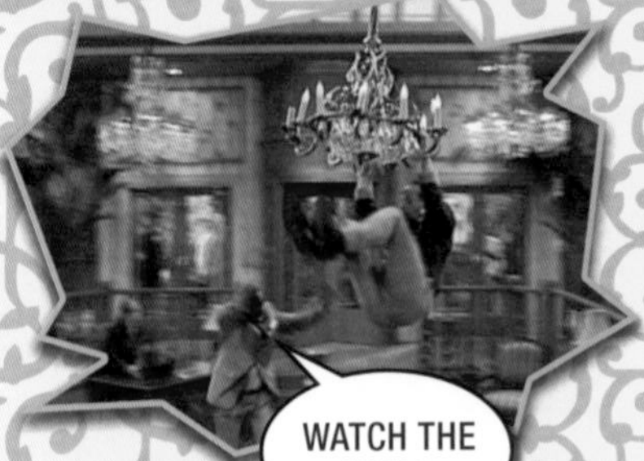
WATCH THE VASE!

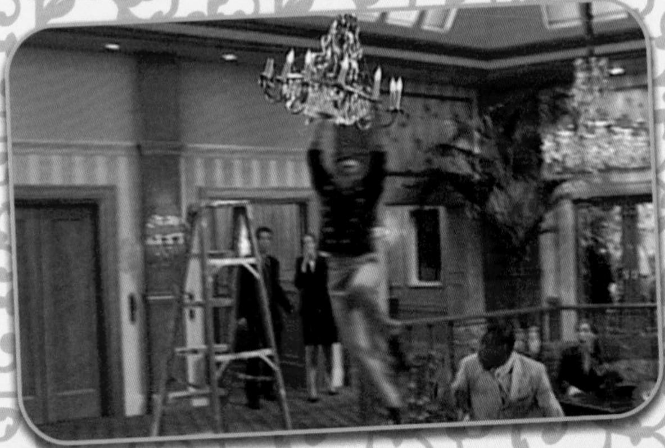

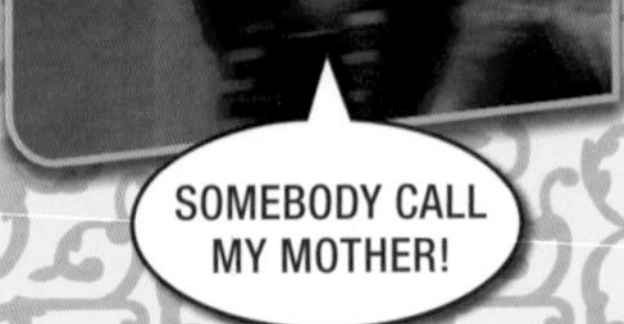
SOMEBODY CALL MY MOTHER!

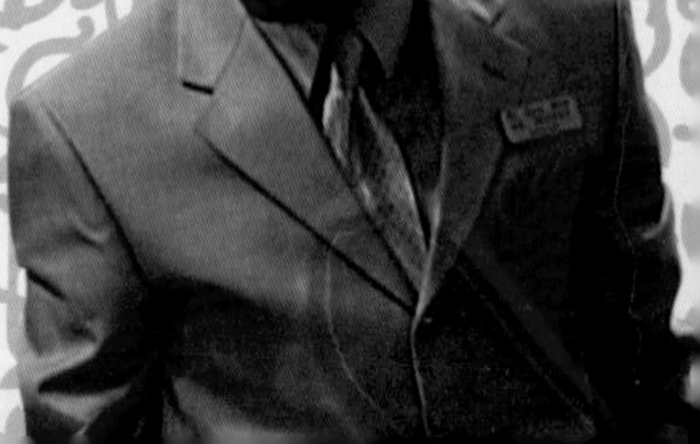
I WANT THOSE KIDS OUT OF HERE.

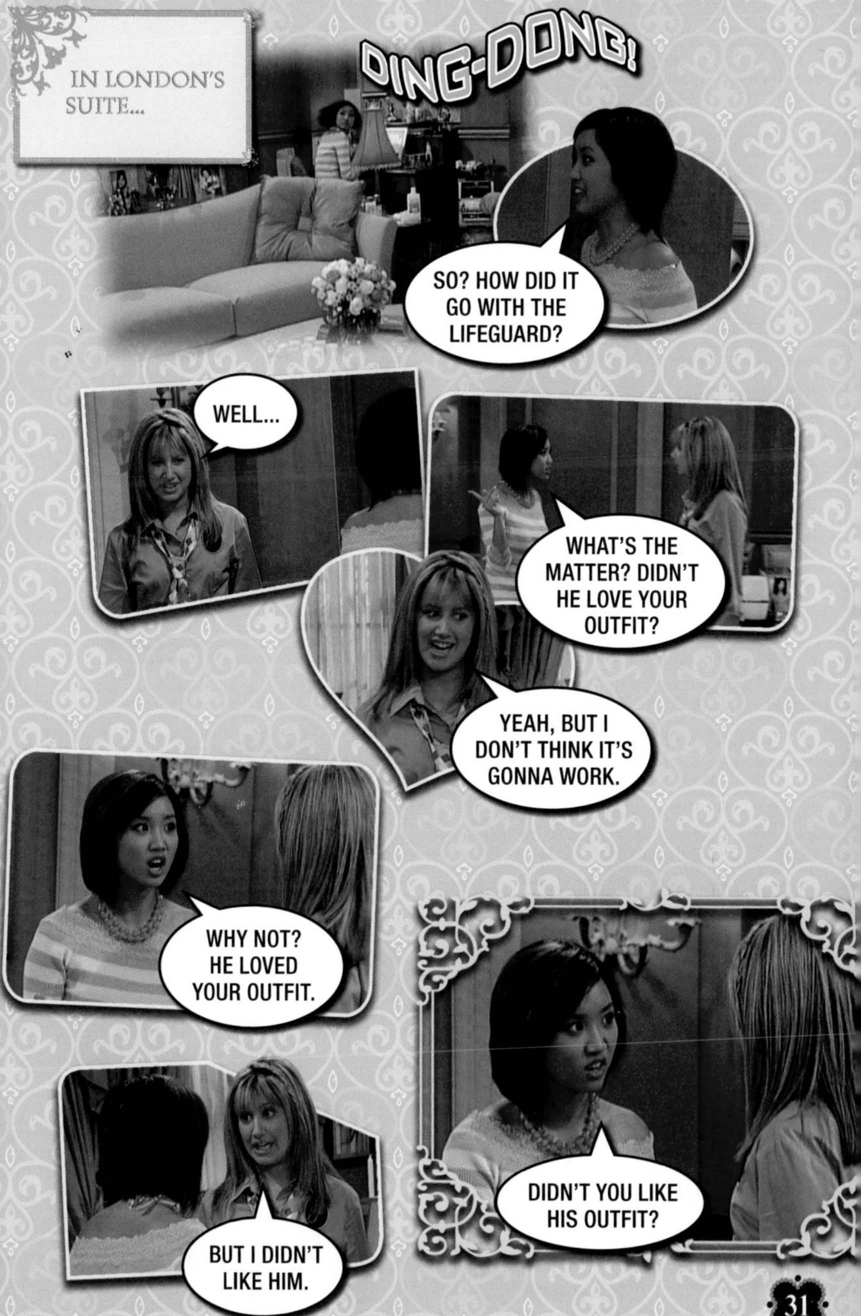
IN LONDON'S SUITE...
DING-DONG!
SO? HOW DID IT GO WITH THE LIFEGUARD?
WELL...
WHAT'S THE MATTER? DIDN'T HE LOVE YOUR OUTFIT?
YEAH, BUT I DON'T THINK IT'S GONNA WORK.
WHY NOT? HE LOVED YOUR OUTFIT.
DIDN'T YOU LIKE HIS OUTFIT?
BUT I DIDN'T LIKE HIM.

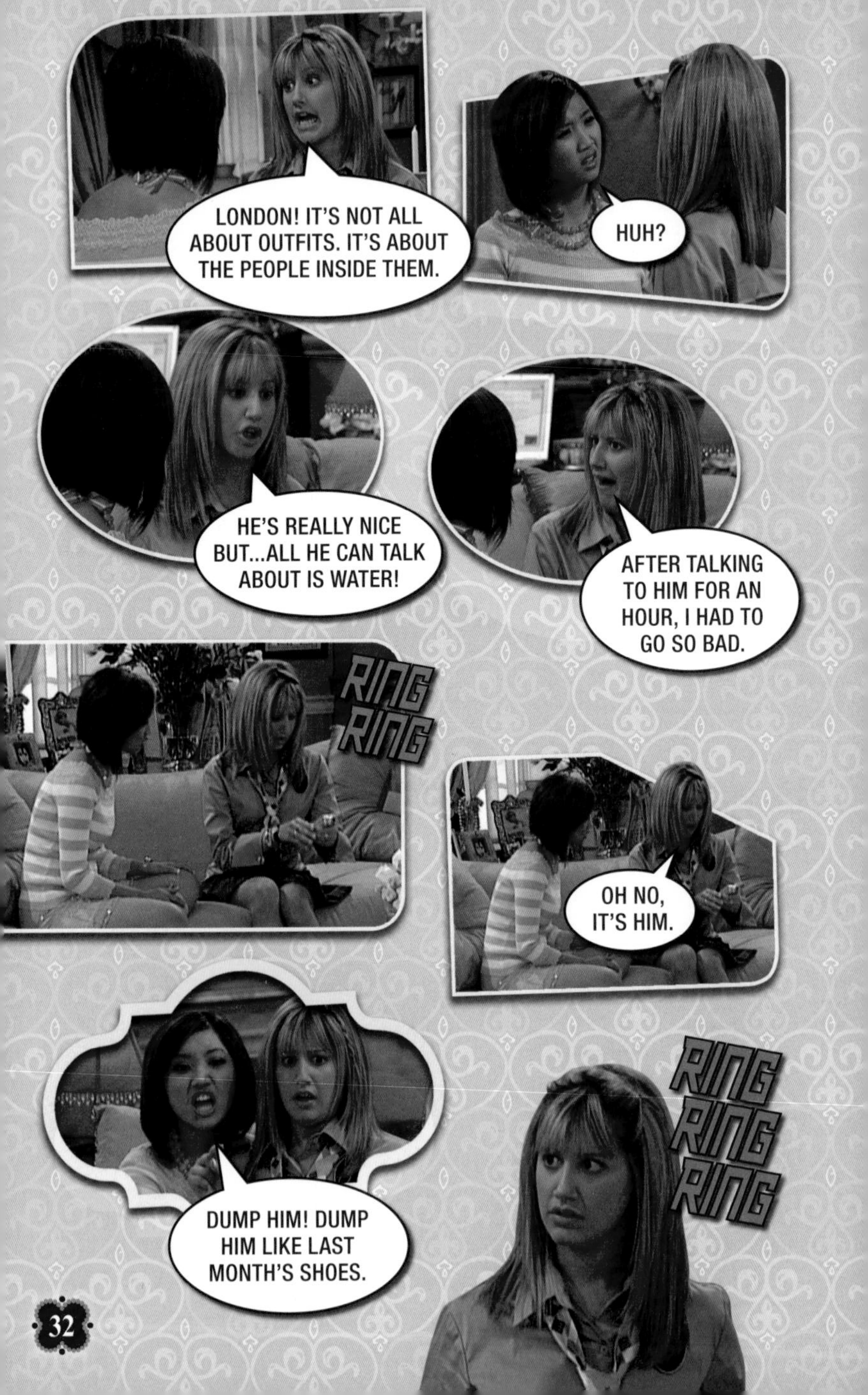
LONDON! IT'S NOT ALL ABOUT OUTFITS. IT'S ABOUT THE PEOPLE INSIDE THEM.
HUH?
HE'S REALLY NICE BUT...ALL HE CAN TALK ABOUT IS WATER!
AFTER TALKING TO HIM FOR AN HOUR, I HAD TO GO SO BAD.
RING RING
OH NO, IT'S HIM.
DUMP HIM! DUMP HIM LIKE LAST MONTH'S SHOES.
RING RING RING

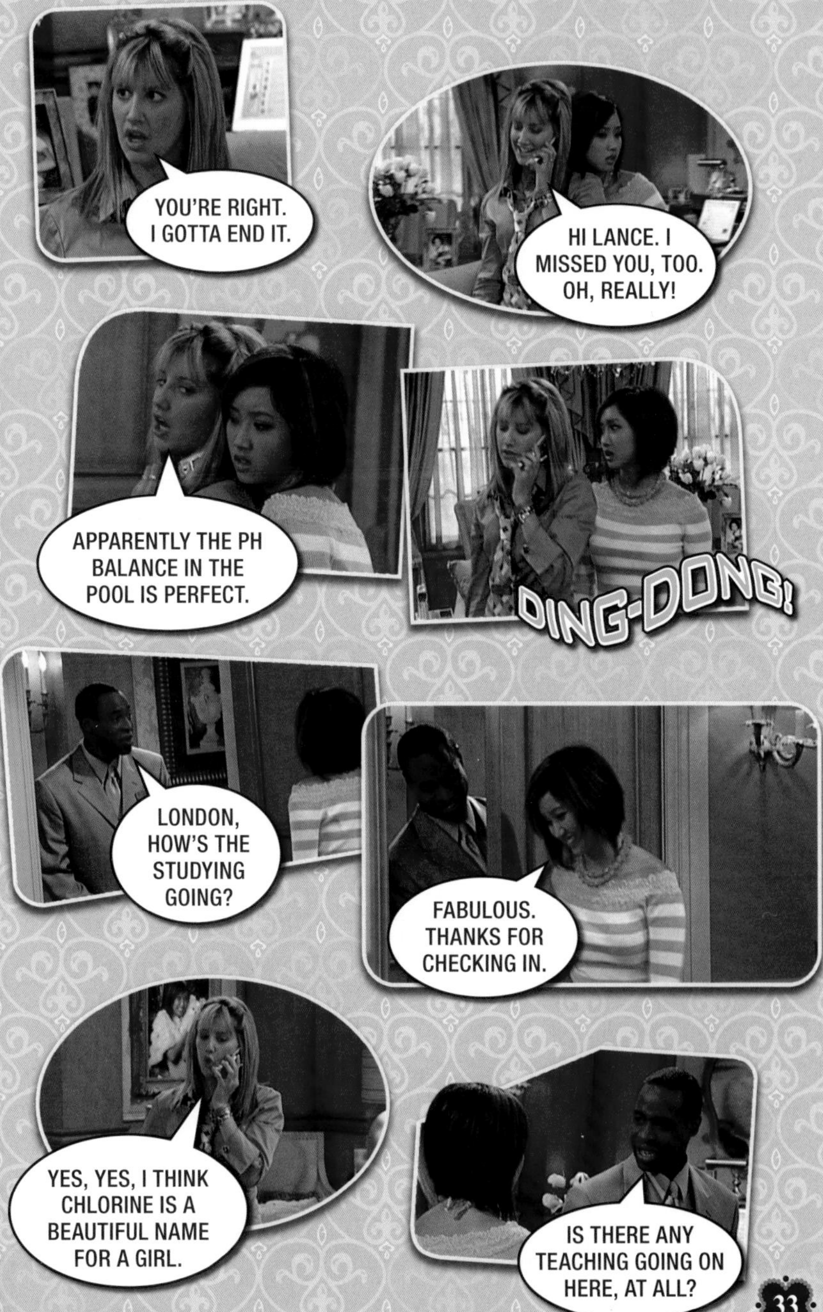
YOU'RE RIGHT. I GOTTA END IT.
HI LANCE. I MISSED YOU, TOO. OH, REALLY!
APPARENTLY THE PH BALANCE IN THE POOL IS PERFECT.
DING-DONG!
LONDON, HOW'S THE STUDYING GOING?
FABULOUS. THANKS FOR CHECKING IN.
YES, YES, I THINK CHLORINE IS A BEAUTIFUL NAME FOR A GIRL.
IS THERE ANY TEACHING GOING ON HERE, AT ALL?

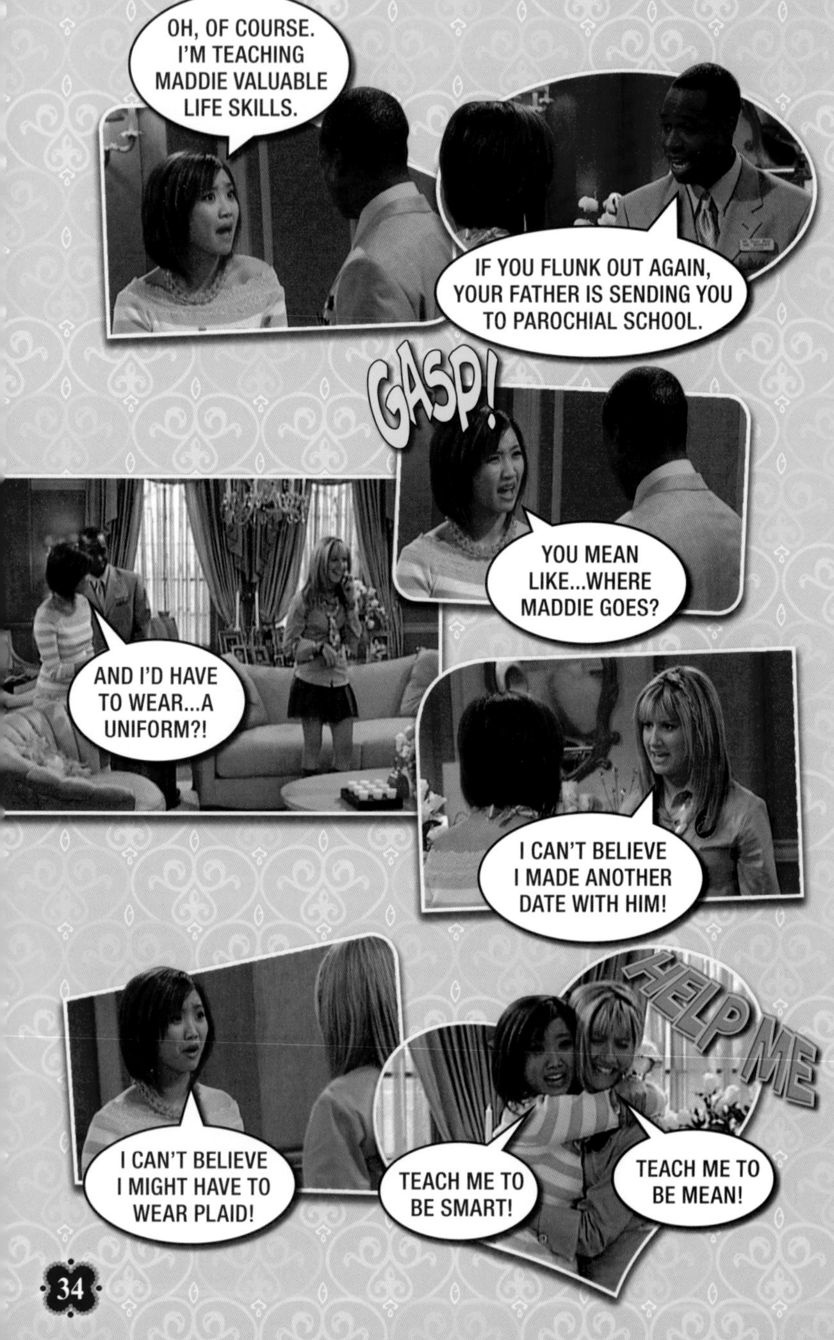
OH, OF COURSE. I'M TEACHING MADDIE VALUABLE LIFE SKILLS.
IF YOU FLUNK OUT AGAIN, YOUR FATHER IS SENDING YOU TO PAROCHIAL SCHOOL.
GASP!
YOU MEAN LIKE...WHERE MADDIE GOES?
AND I'D HAVE TO WEAR...A UNIFORM?!
I CAN'T BELIEVE I MADE ANOTHER DATE WITH HIM!
I CAN'T BELIEVE I MIGHT HAVE TO WEAR PLAID!
HELP ME
TEACH ME TO BE SMART!
TEACH ME TO BE MEAN!

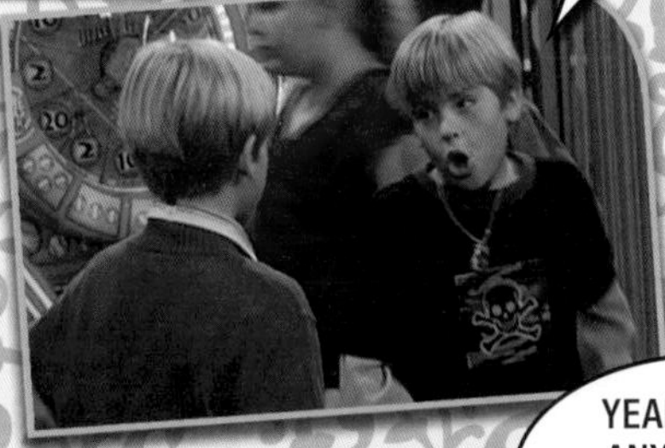
IN THE GAME ROOM...
ALL OF THE A-LIST KIDS ARE HERE.

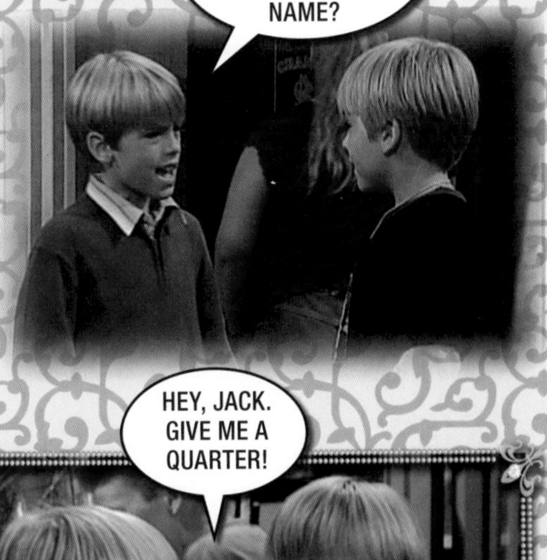
YEAH, BUT DO ANY OF THEM EVEN KNOW YOUR NAME?

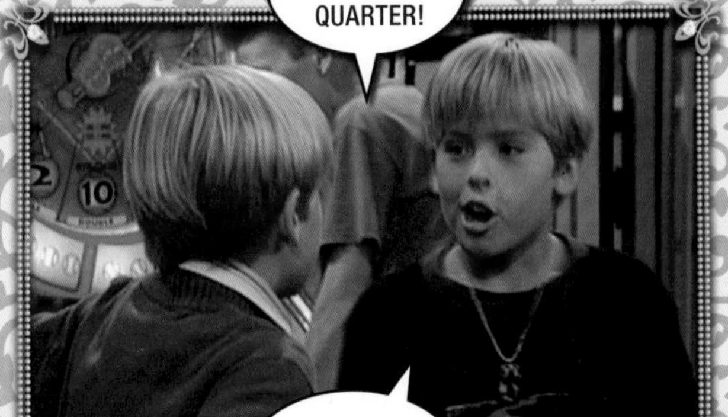
HEY, JACK. GIVE ME A QUARTER!
SEE? OFF BY ONE LETTER.

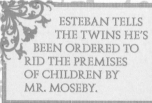
ESTEBAN TELLS THE TWINS HE'S BEEN ORDERED TO RID THE PREMISES OF CHILDREN BY MR. MOSEBY.

uh-oh

WE CAN'T ASK THEM TO LEAVE, THEY'RE OUR FRIENDS.

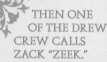
THEN ONE OF THE DREW CREW CALLS ZACK "ZEEK."

36

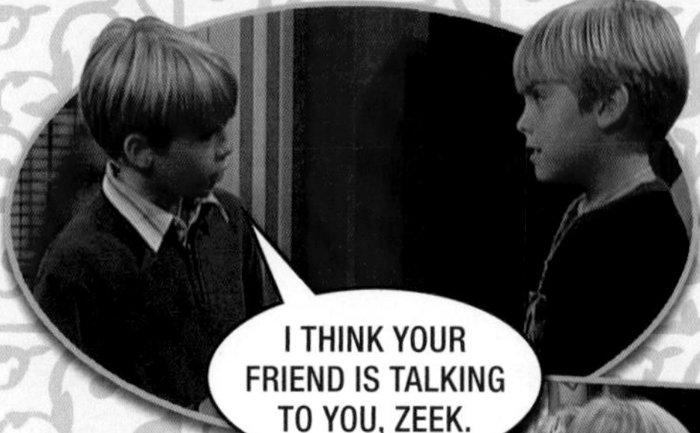
I THINK YOUR FRIEND IS TALKING TO YOU, ZEEK.

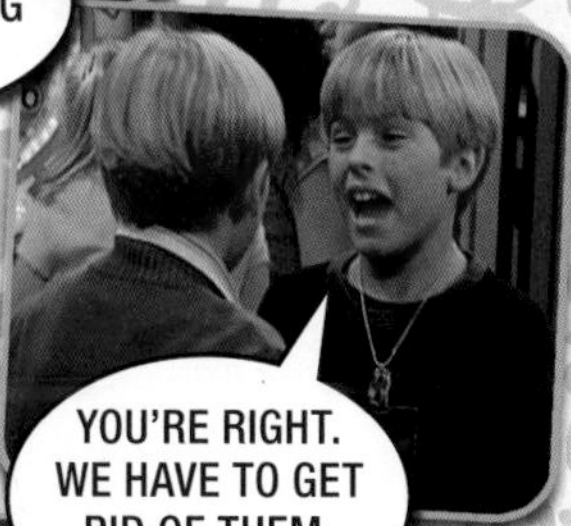
YOU'RE RIGHT. WE HAVE TO GET RID OF THEM. BUT HOW?

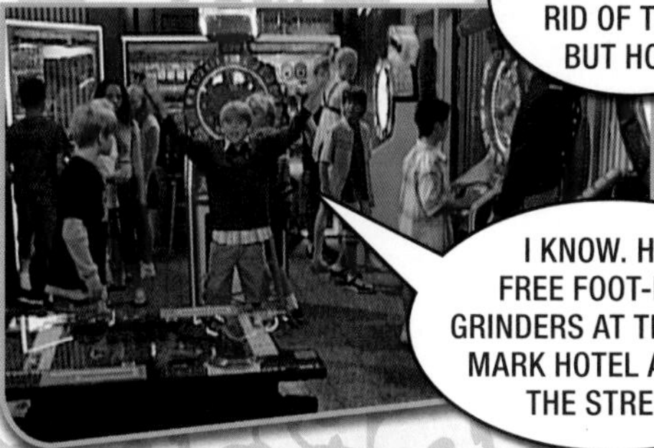
I KNOW. HEY! FREE FOOT-LONG GRINDERS AT THE SAINT MARK HOTEL ACROSS THE STREET!

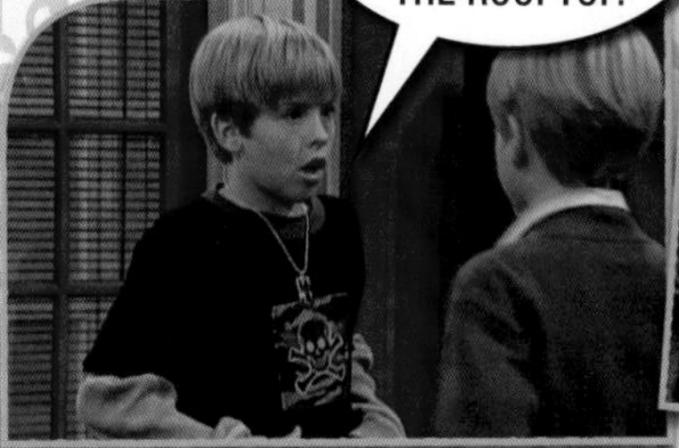
EXCELLENT, I'LL CLEAR OUT THE LOBBY, YOU GET THE ROOFTOP.

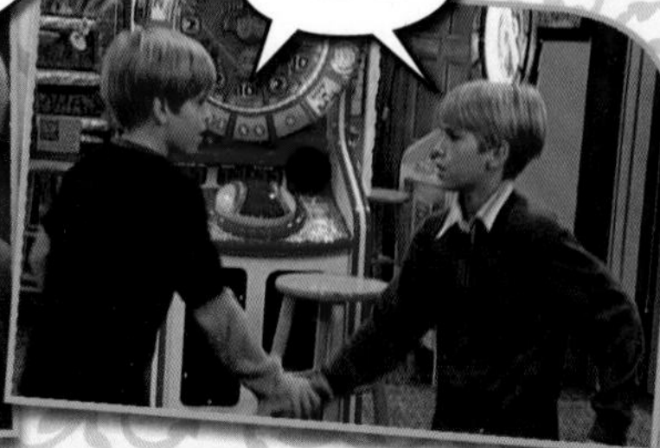
BREAK!

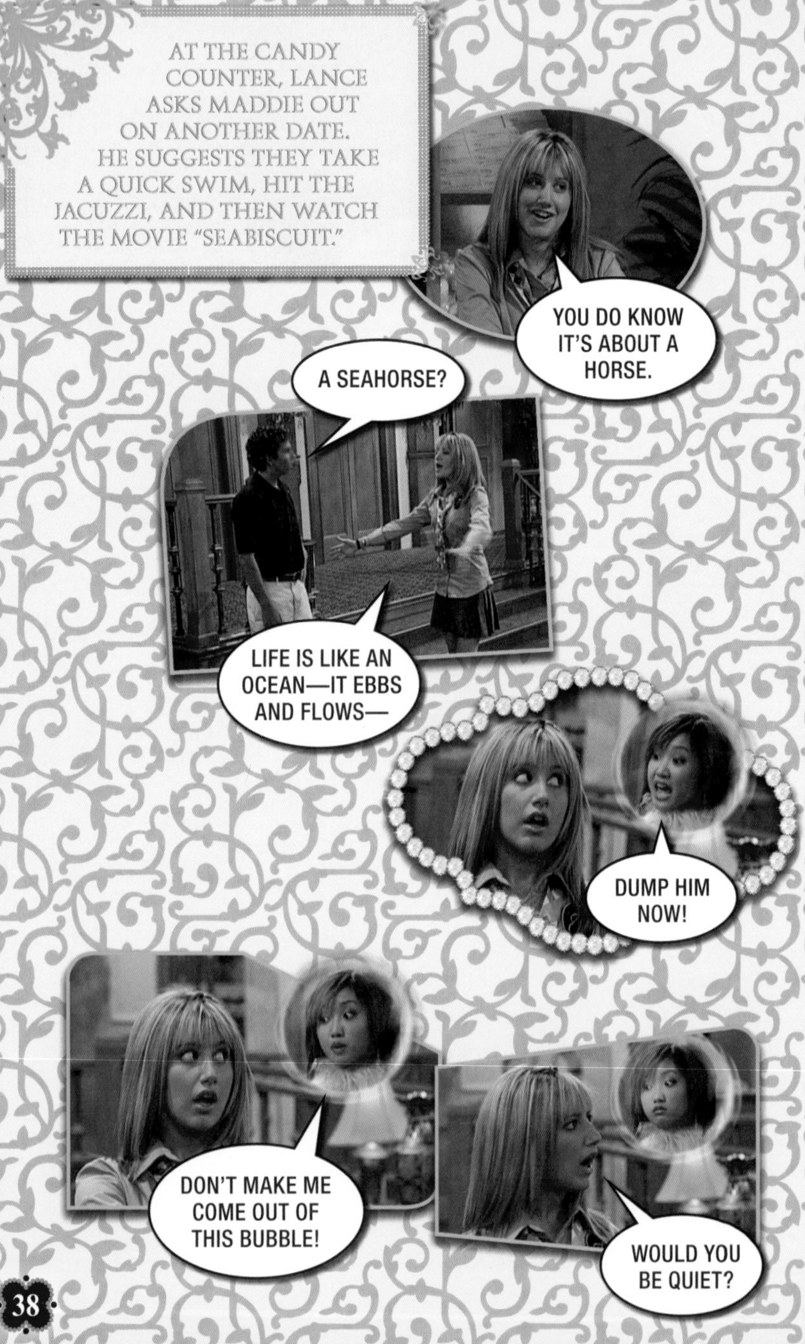
AT THE CANDY COUNTER, LANCE ASKS MADDIE OUT ON ANOTHER DATE. HE SUGGESTS THEY TAKE A QUICK SWIM, HIT THE JACUZZI, AND THEN WATCH THE MOVIE "SEABISCUIT."
YOU DO KNOW IT'S ABOUT A HORSE.
A SEAHORSE?
LIFE IS LIKE AN OCEAN—IT EBBS AND FLOWS—
DUMP HIM NOW!
DON'T MAKE ME COME OUT OF THIS BUBBLE!
WOULD YOU BE QUIET?

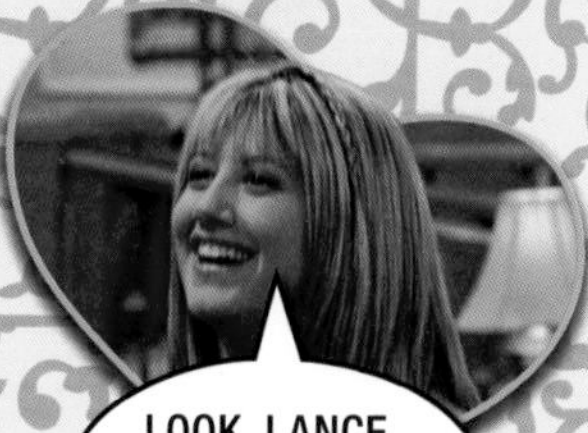
LOOK, LANCE... LIFE IS LIKE A RIVER—

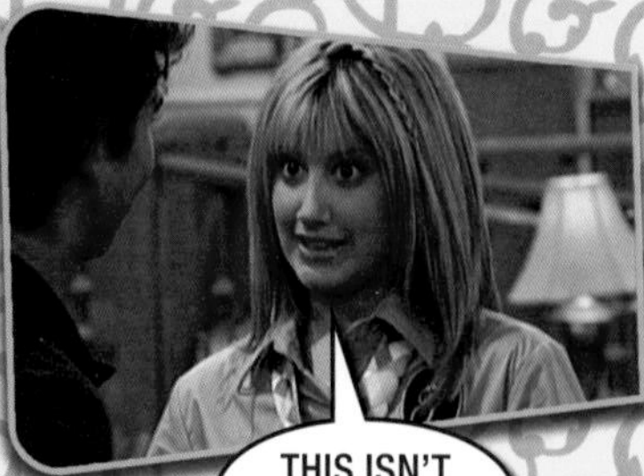
THIS ISN'T WORKING.

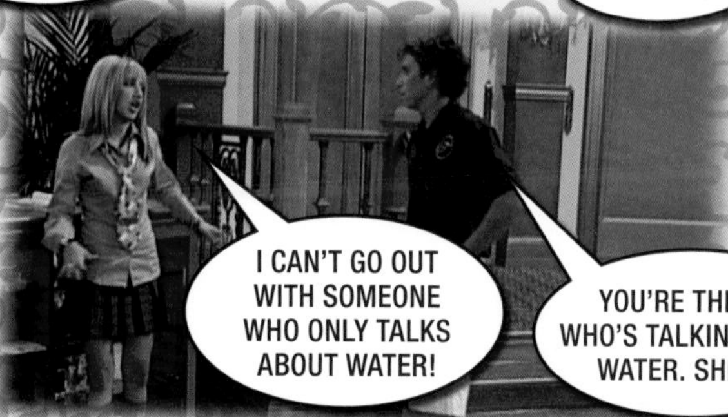
I CAN'T GO OUT WITH SOMEONE WHO ONLY TALKS ABOUT WATER!
YOU'RE THE ONE WHO'S TALKING ABOUT WATER. SHEESH.

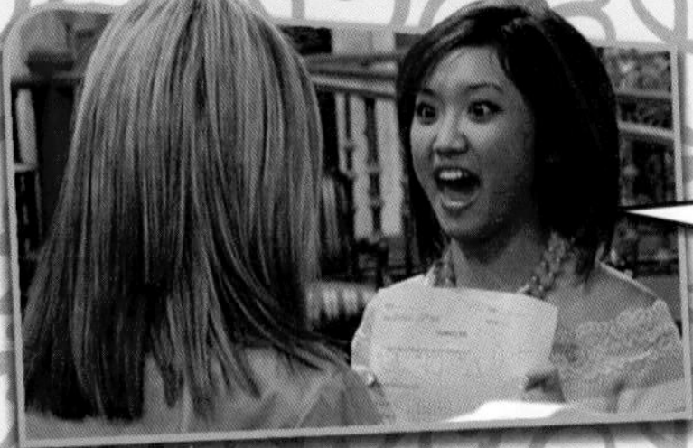
GOOD NEWS! I GOT A D-PLUS IN MATH!

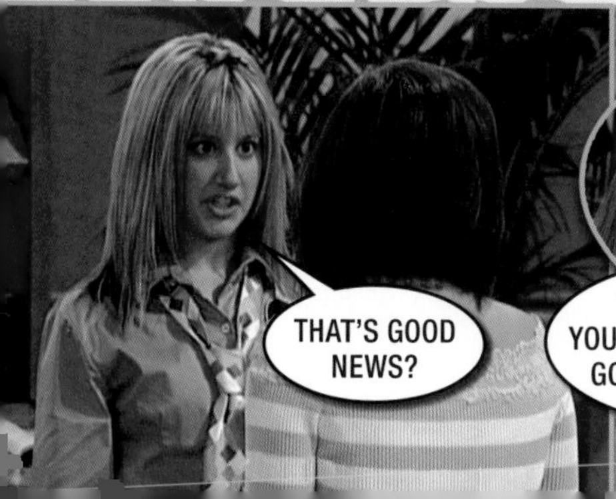
THAT'S GOOD NEWS?

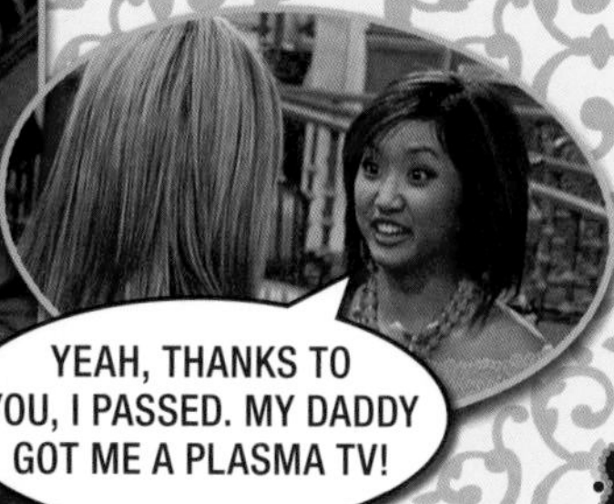
YEAH, THANKS TO YOU, I PASSED. MY DADDY GOT ME A PLASMA TV!

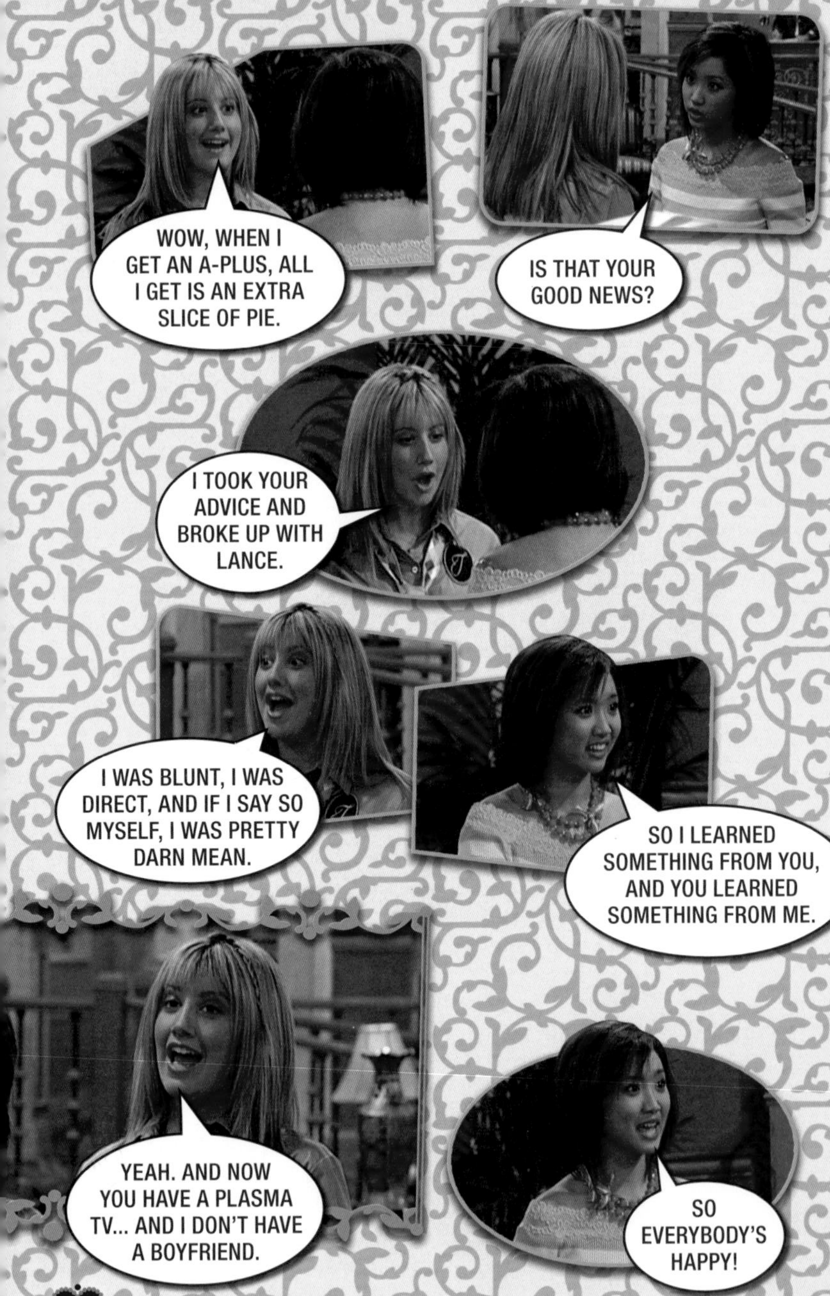
WOW, WHEN I GET AN A-PLUS, ALL I GET IS AN EXTRA SLICE OF PIE.
IS THAT YOUR GOOD NEWS?
I TOOK YOUR ADVICE AND BROKE UP WITH LANCE.
I WAS BLUNT, I WAS DIRECT, AND IF I SAY SO MYSELF, I WAS PRETTY DARN MEAN.
SO I LEARNED SOMETHING FROM YOU, AND YOU LEARNED SOMETHING FROM ME.
YEAH. AND NOW YOU HAVE A PLASMA TV... AND I DON'T HAVE A BOYFRIEND.
SO EVERYBODY'S HAPPY!

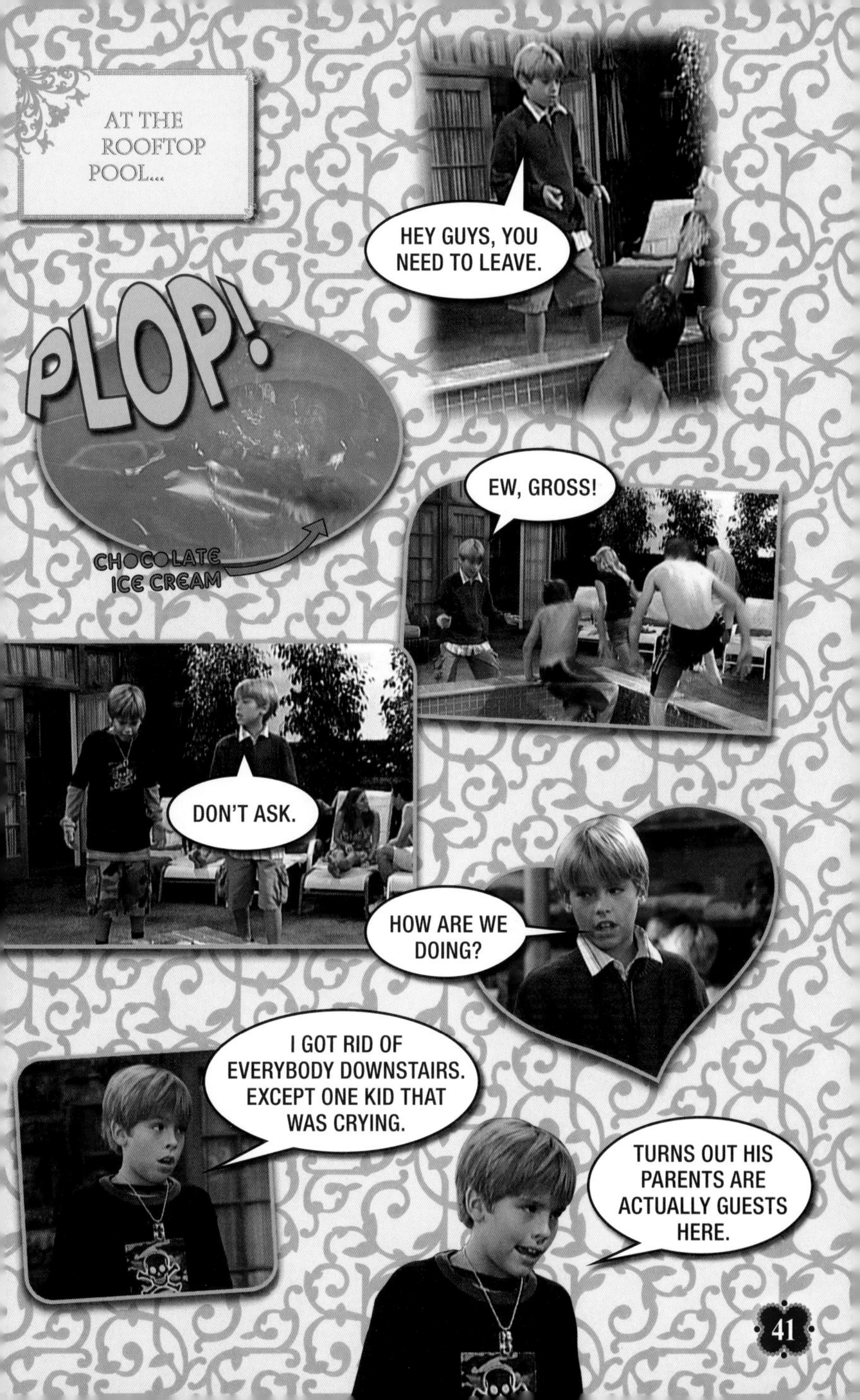
AT THE ROOFTOP POOL...
HEY GUYS, YOU NEED TO LEAVE.
PLOP!
CHOCOLATE ICE CREAM
EW, GROSS!
DON'T ASK.
HOW ARE WE DOING?
I GOT RID OF EVERYBODY DOWNSTAIRS. EXCEPT ONE KID THAT WAS CRYING.
TURNS OUT HIS PARENTS ARE ACTUALLY GUESTS HERE.

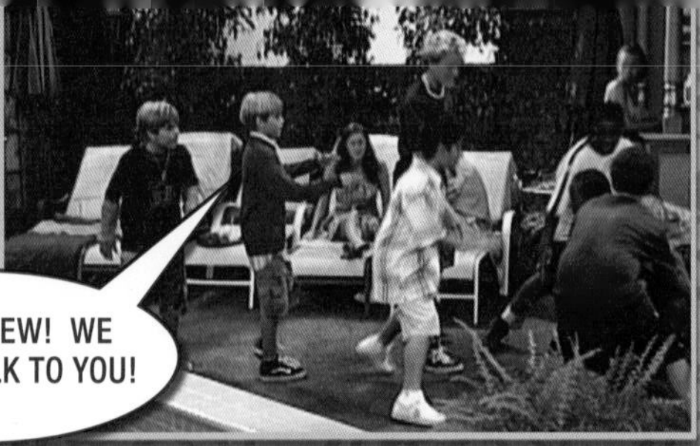
DREW! DREW! WE NEED TO TALK TO YOU!

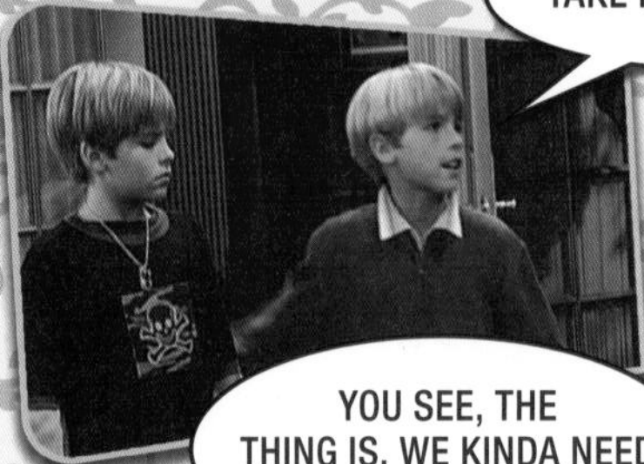
TAKE IT AWAY, ZACK.

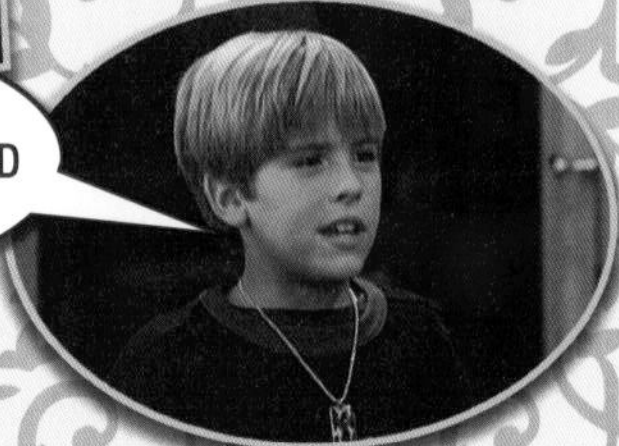
YOU SEE, THE THING IS, WE KINDA NEED YA TO LEAVE.

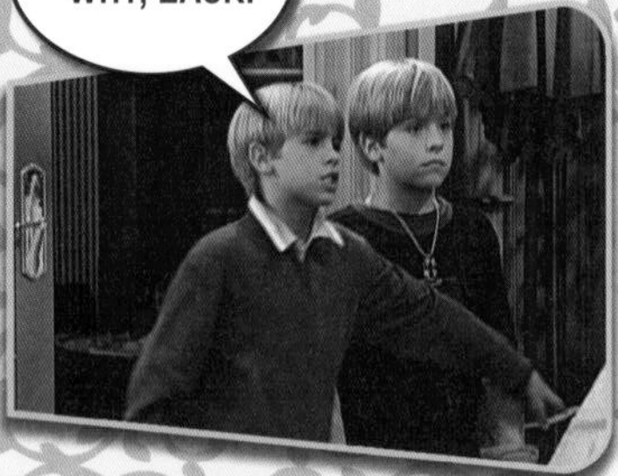
TELL HIM WHY, ZACK.

DREW SAYS IF HE AND HIS FRIENDS LEAVE, THEY'RE NOT COMING BACK...SO THE TWINS WILL HAVE TO HANG WITH THOSE "DWEEBS," MAX AND SILKWORM.

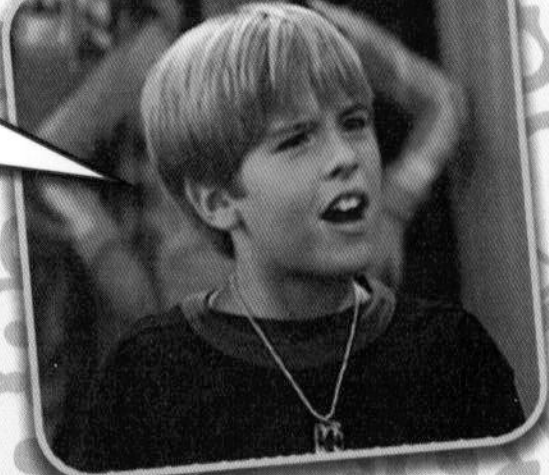
HIS NAME IS TAPEWORM. AND HE'S OUR FRIEND. AND SO IS THE OTHER DWEEB.

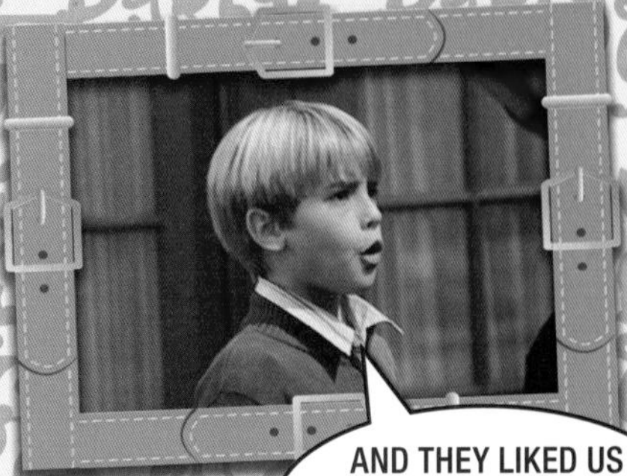
AND THEY LIKED US BEFORE THEY KNEW WE HAD THIS COOL PLACE.

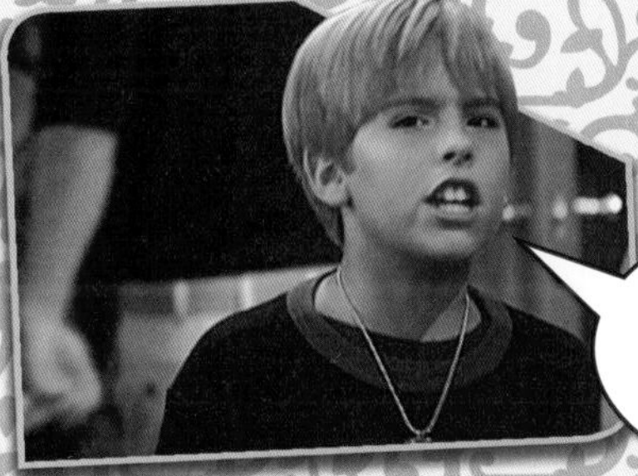
YOU MADE US DITCH THEM, SO NOW WE'RE DITCHING YOU. GIVE ME BACK THE BALL, DREW.

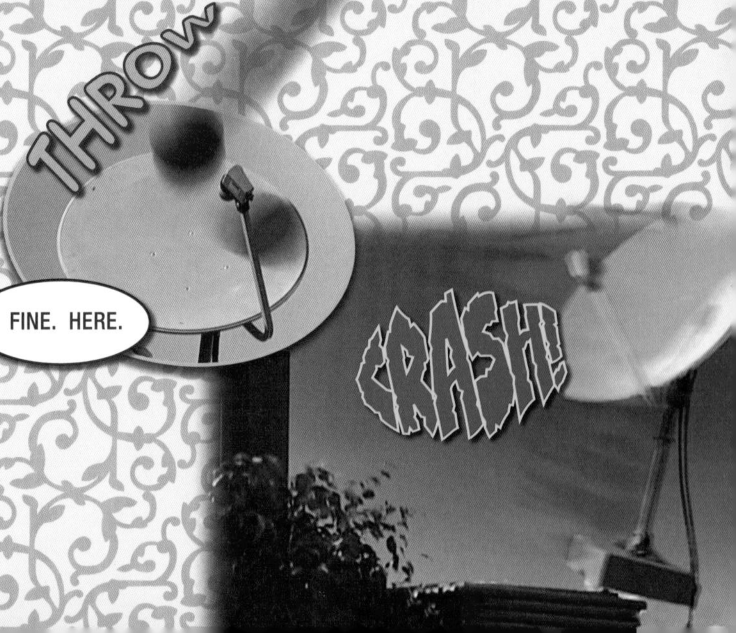
THROW
FINE. HERE.
CRASH!

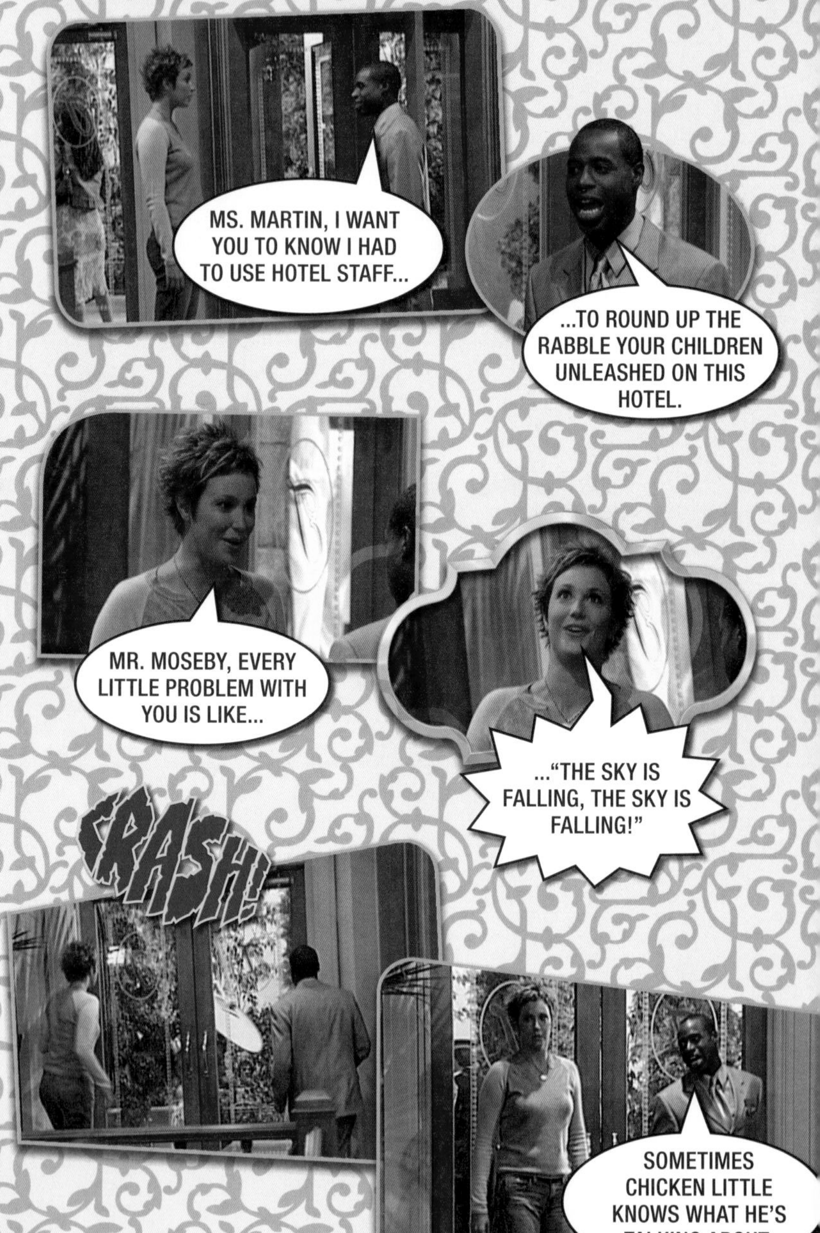
MS. MARTIN, I WANT YOU TO KNOW I HAD TO USE HOTEL STAFF...
...TO ROUND UP THE RABBLE YOUR CHILDREN UNLEASHED ON THIS HOTEL.
MR. MOSEBY, EVERY LITTLE PROBLEM WITH YOU IS LIKE...
..."THE SKY IS FALLING, THE SKY IS FALLING!"
CRASH!
SOMETIMES CHICKEN LITTLE KNOWS WHAT HE'S TALKING ABOUT.

ZACK AND CODY TRY TO HOLD UP THE SATELLITE DISH DREW BROKE.

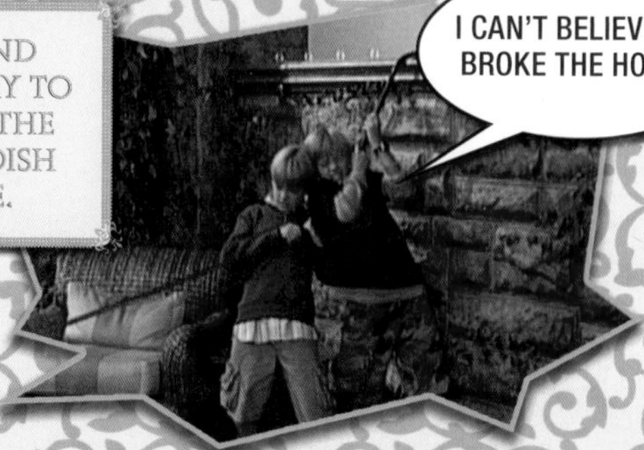
I CAN'T BELIEVE WE BROKE THE HOTEL.

MAX AND TAPEWORM OFFER TO HELP.

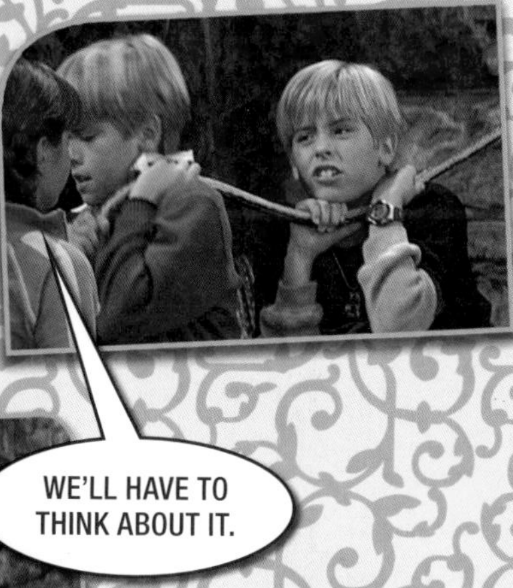

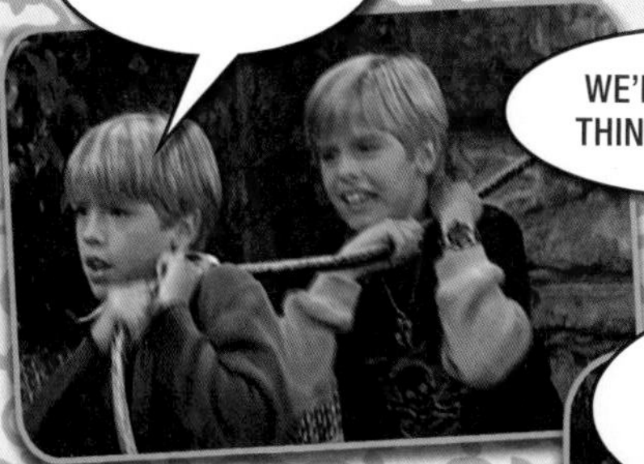
SO... WE'RE FRIENDS AGAIN?
WE'LL HAVE TO THINK ABOUT IT.

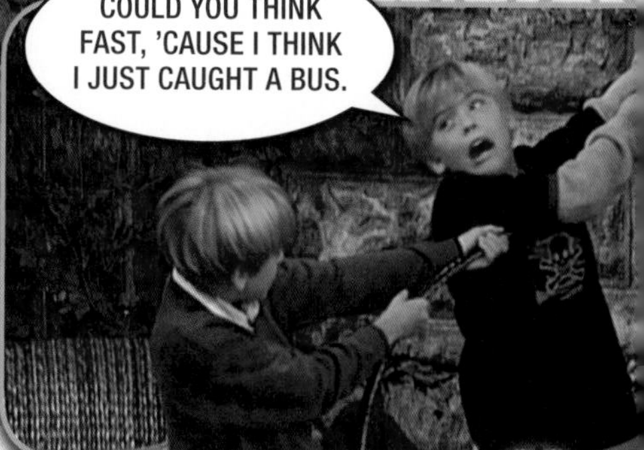
COULD YOU THINK FAST, 'CAUSE I THINK I JUST CAUGHT A BUS.

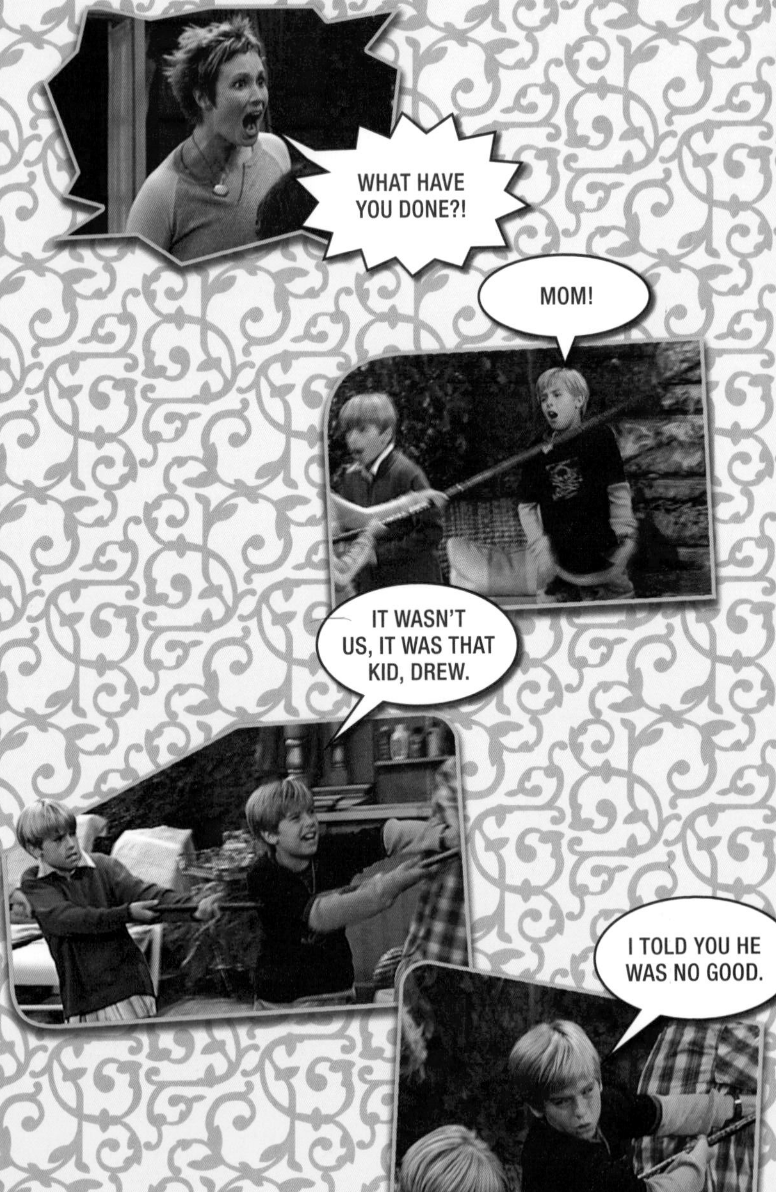
WHAT HAVE YOU DONE?!
MOM!
IT WASN'T US, IT WAS THAT KID, DREW.
I TOLD YOU HE WAS NO GOOD.

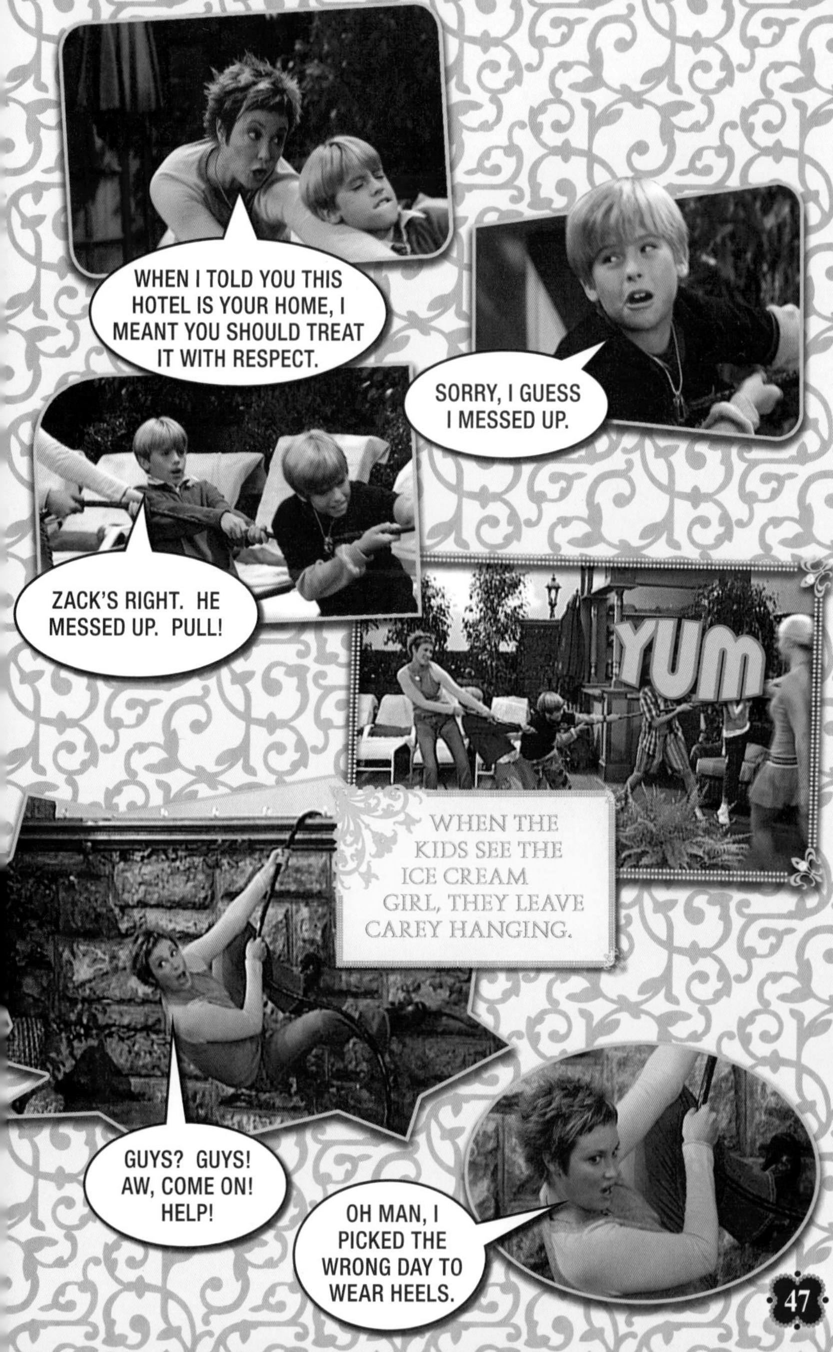
WHEN I TOLD YOU THIS HOTEL IS YOUR HOME, I MEANT YOU SHOULD TREAT IT WITH RESPECT.
SORRY, I GUESS I MESSED UP.
ZACK'S RIGHT. HE MESSED UP. PULL!
YUM
WHEN THE KIDS SEE THE ICE CREAM GIRL, THEY LEAVE CAREY HANGING.
GUYS? GUYS! AW, COME ON! HELP!
OH MAN, I PICKED THE WRONG DAY TO WEAR HEELS.

LATER, AT THE ROOFTOP POOL...

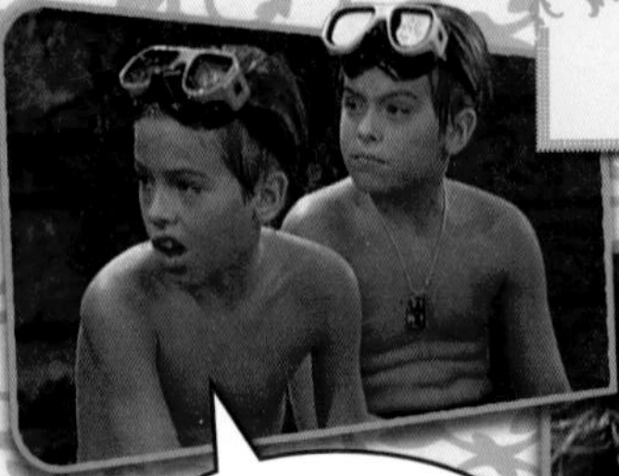
THIS IS THE WORST PUNISHMENT WE EVER GOT.

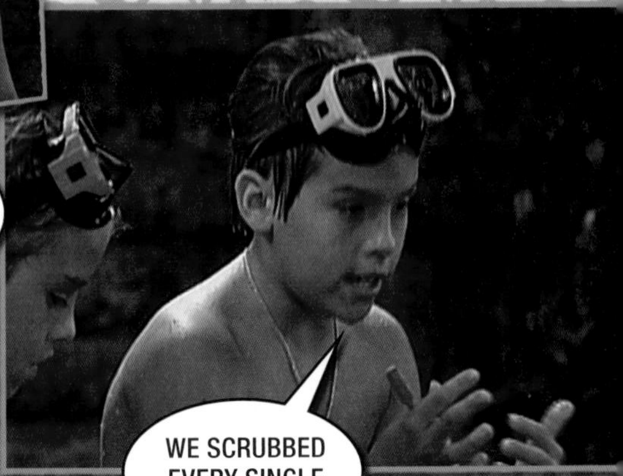
WE SCRUBBED EVERY SINGLE TILE.

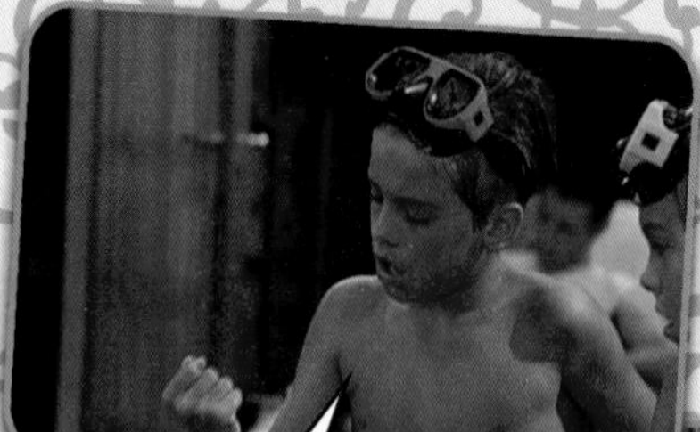
I CAN'T UNCURL MY FINGERS.

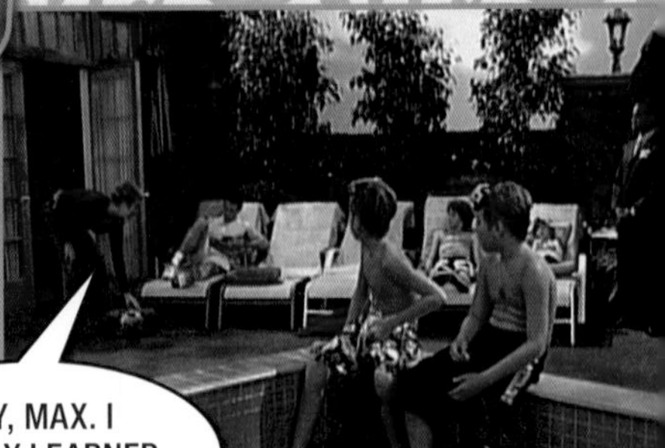
HEY, MAX. I FINALLY LEARNED THAT MOVE.

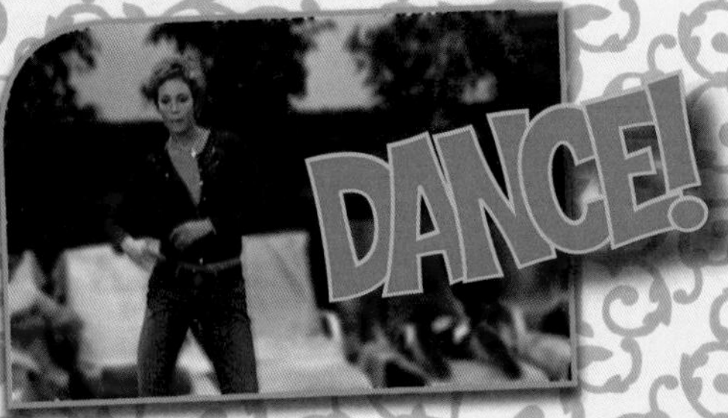
DANCE!

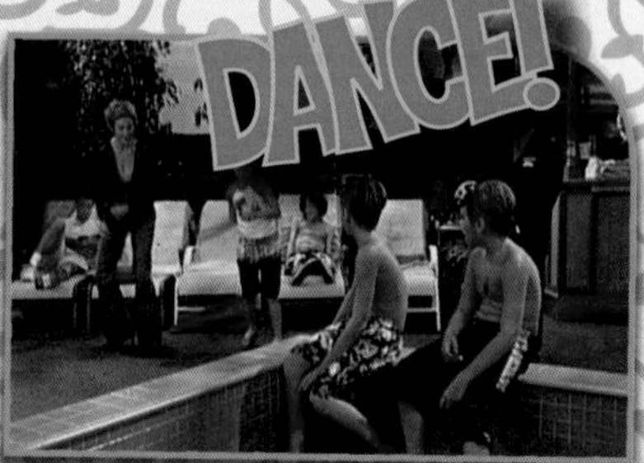
DANCE!

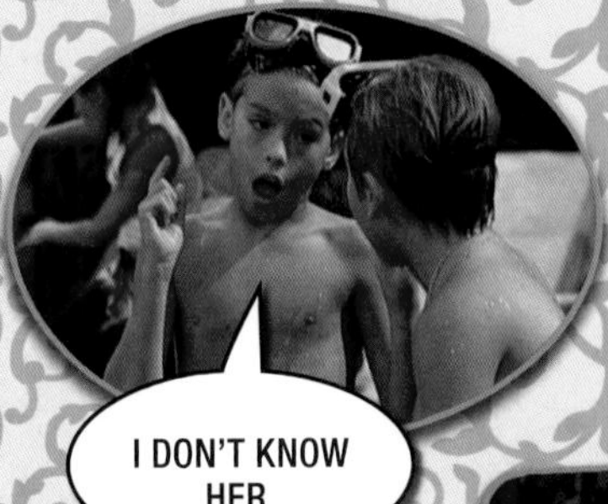
I DON'T KNOW HER.

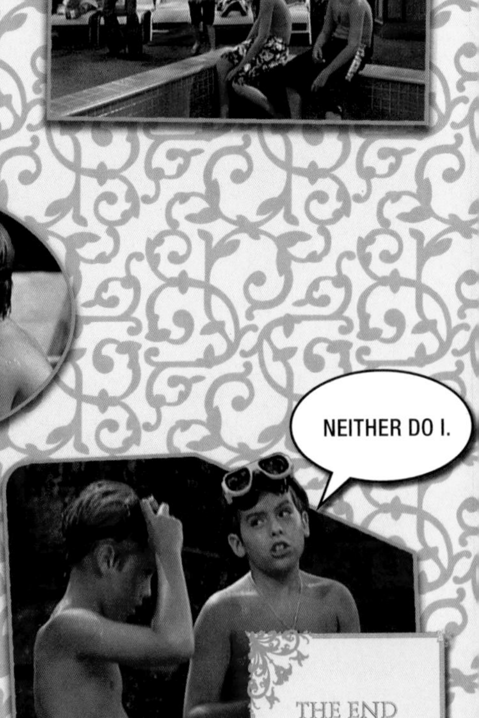
NEITHER DO I.
THE END

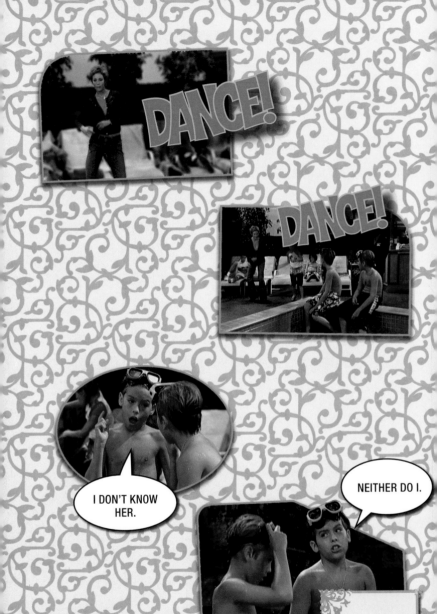

Disney

The Suite Life of Zack & Cody

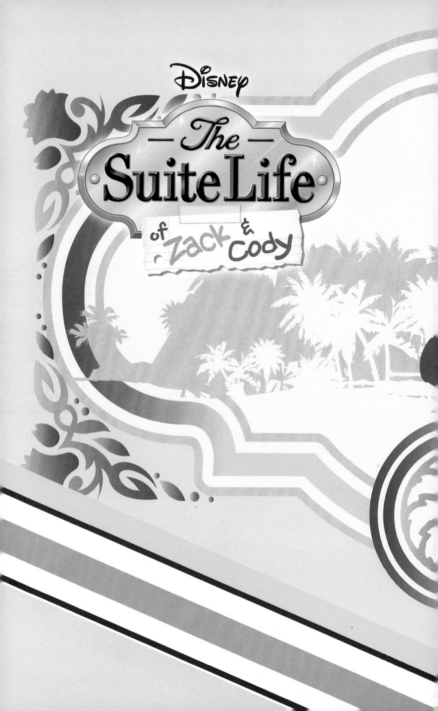

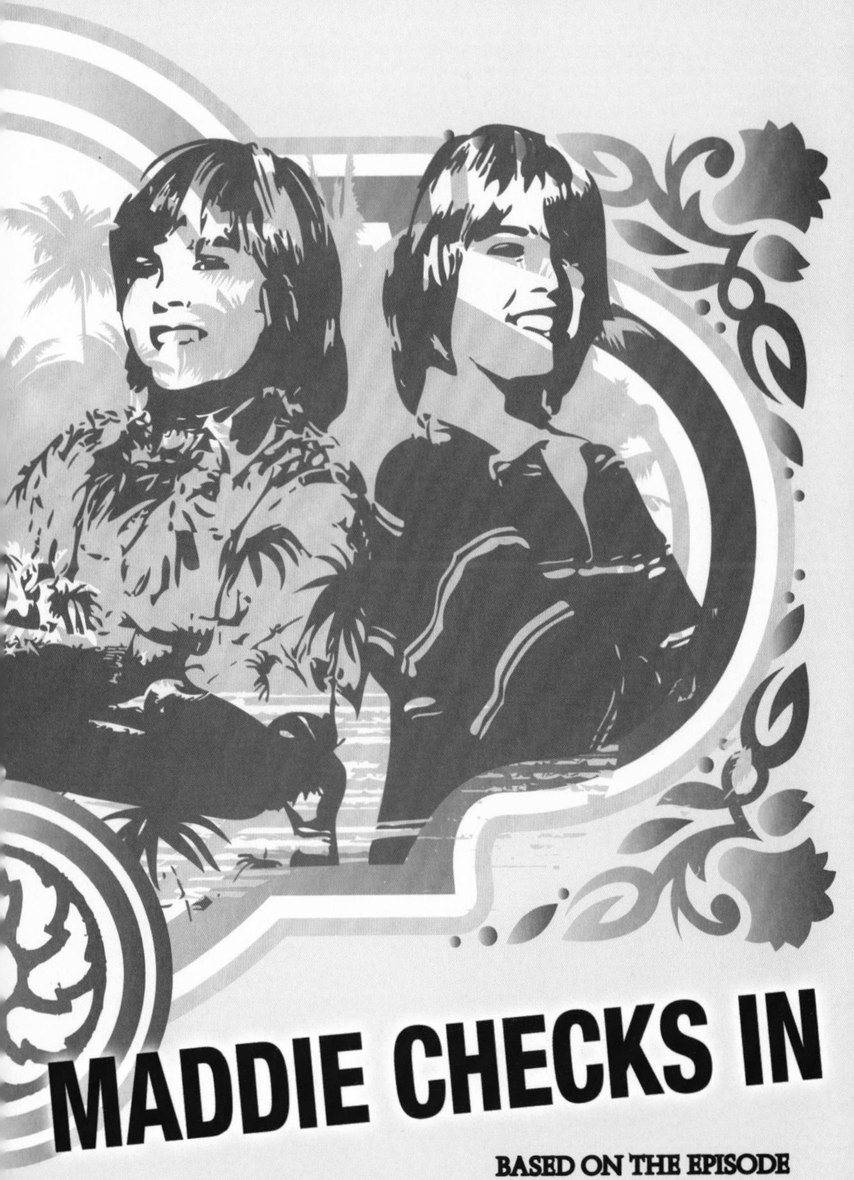

MADDIE CHECKS IN

BASED ON THE EPISODE
WRITTEN BY DANNY KALLIS & JIM GEOGHAN

AT THE CANDY COUNTER...

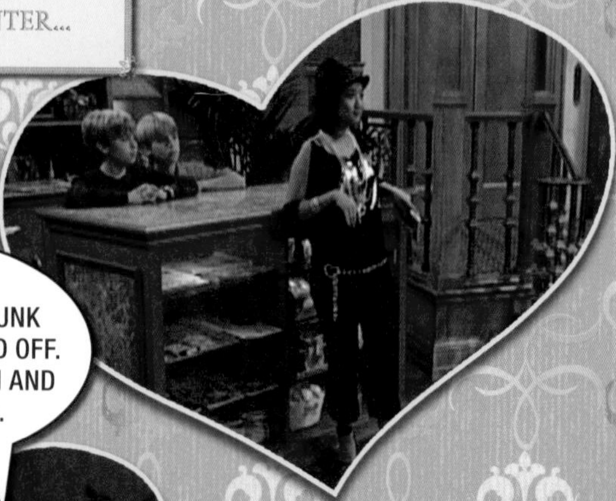

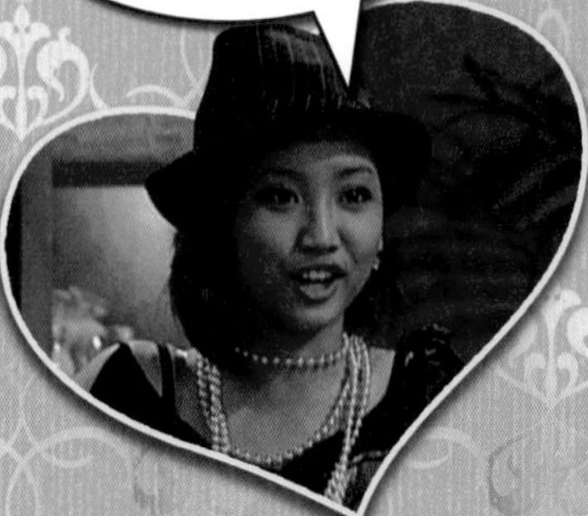
MM-MM, LOOK WHAT THE HUNK FAIRY JUST DROPPED OFF. JASON HARRINGTON AND KYLE LAWFORD.

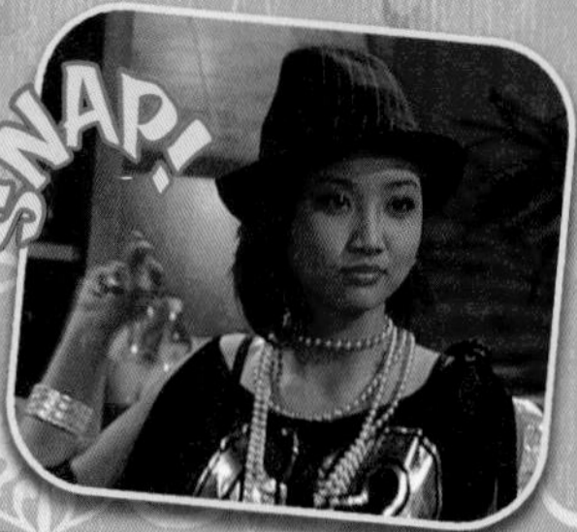
SNAP!

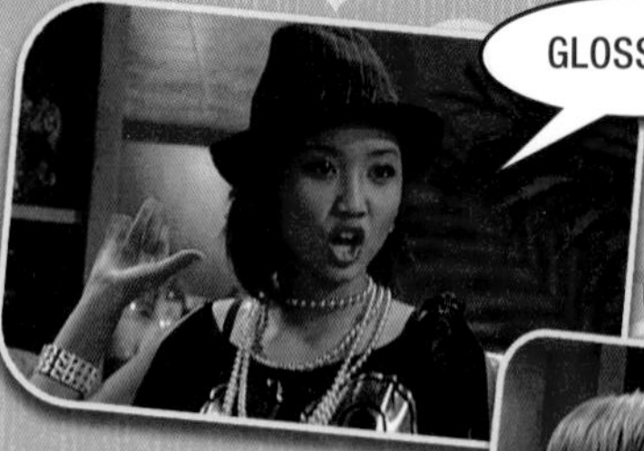
GLOSS ME!

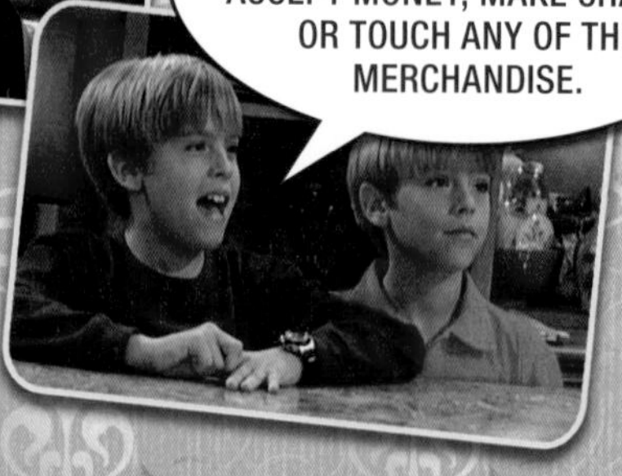
SORRY, WE'RE WATCHING THE COUNTER FOR MADDIE. WE'RE NOT ALLOWED TO ACCEPT MONEY, MAKE CHANGE, OR TOUCH ANY OF THE MERCHANDISE.

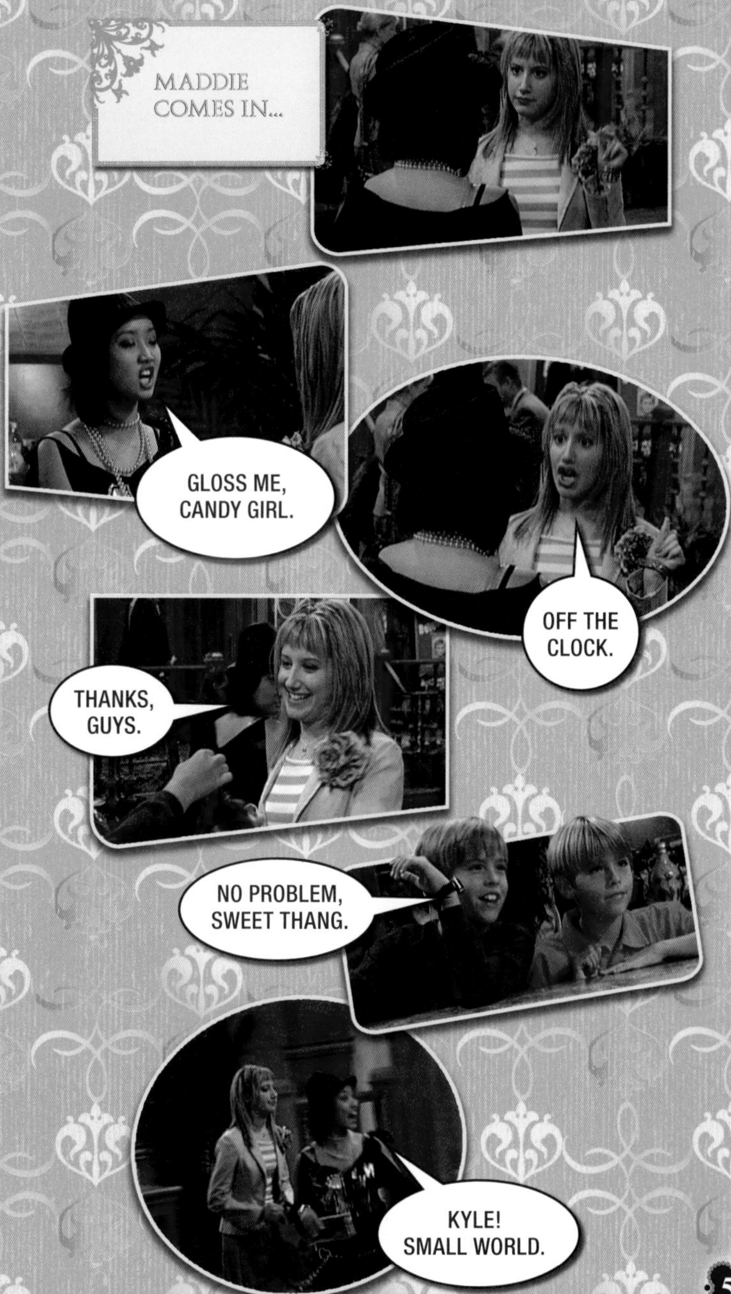
MADDIE COMES IN...
GLOSS ME, CANDY GIRL.
OFF THE CLOCK.
THANKS, GUYS.
NO PROBLEM, SWEET THANG.
KYLE! SMALL WORLD.

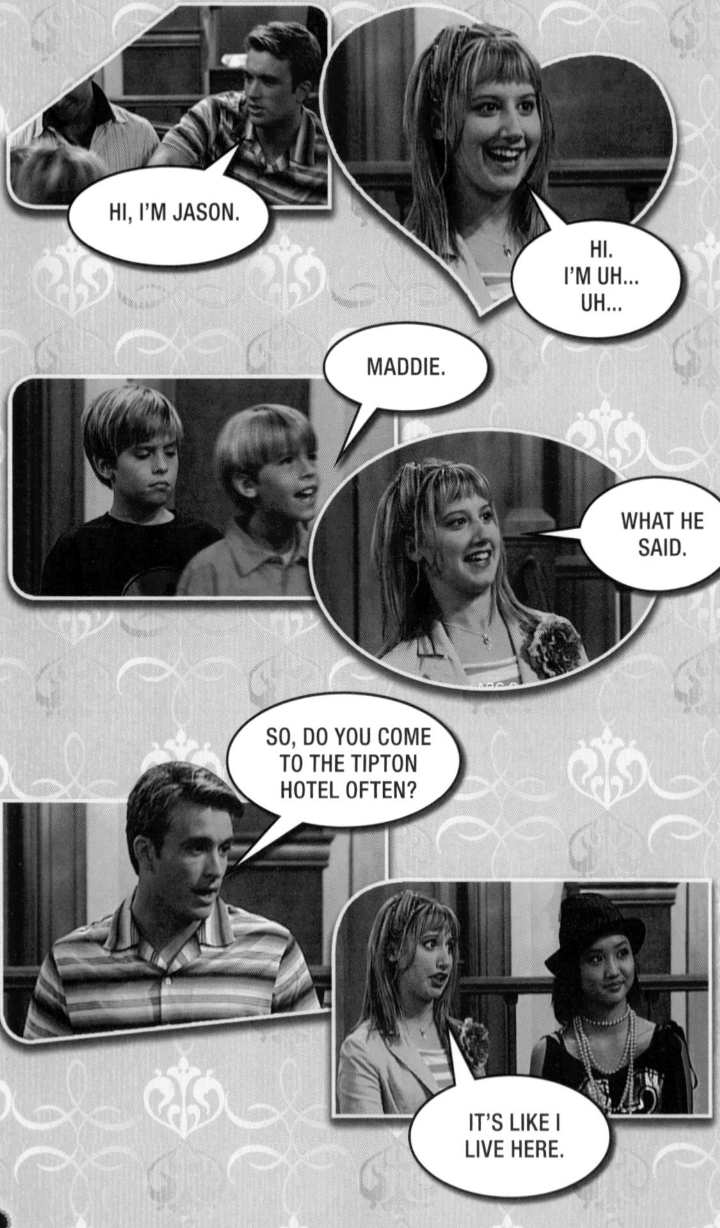
HI, I'M JASON.
HI. I'M UH... UH...
MADDIE.
WHAT HE SAID.
SO, DO YOU COME TO THE TIPTON HOTEL OFTEN?
IT'S LIKE I LIVE HERE.

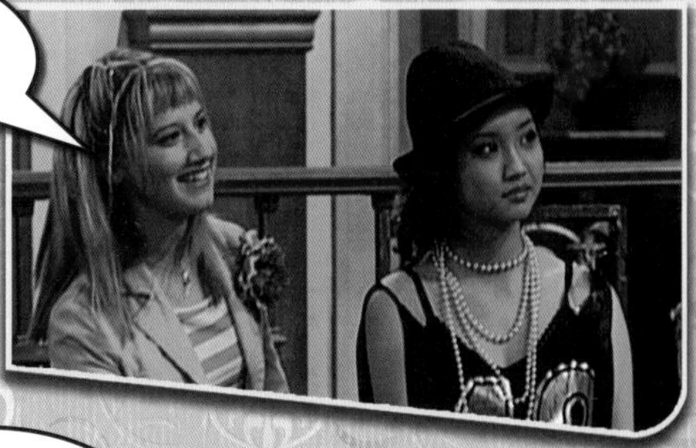
WELL, AS WE SAY, GOTTA JET. NICE TO MEET YOU.

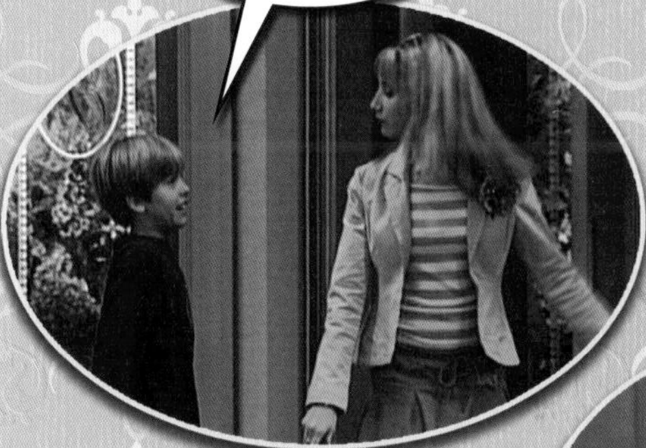
YOU DON'T REALLY LIKE THAT GUY, DO YOU?

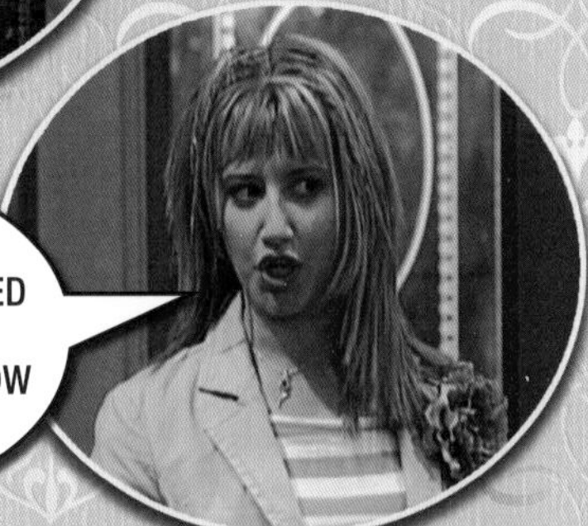
HE'S CUTE, BUT I'VE WORKED HERE LONG ENOUGH TO KNOW HIS TYPE.

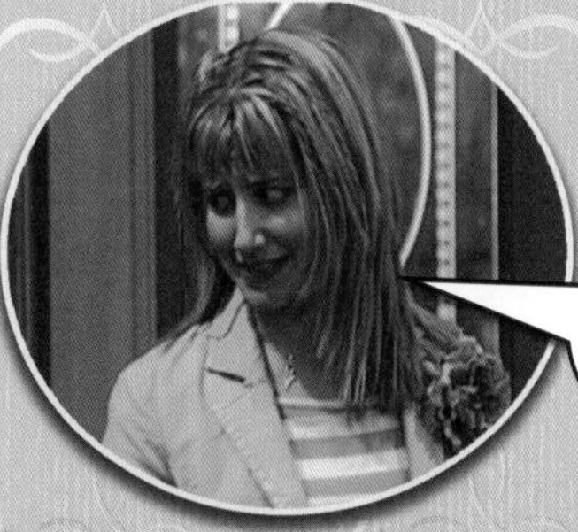
RICH PEOPLE DON'T CARE ABOUT ANYTHING BUT THEMSELVES.

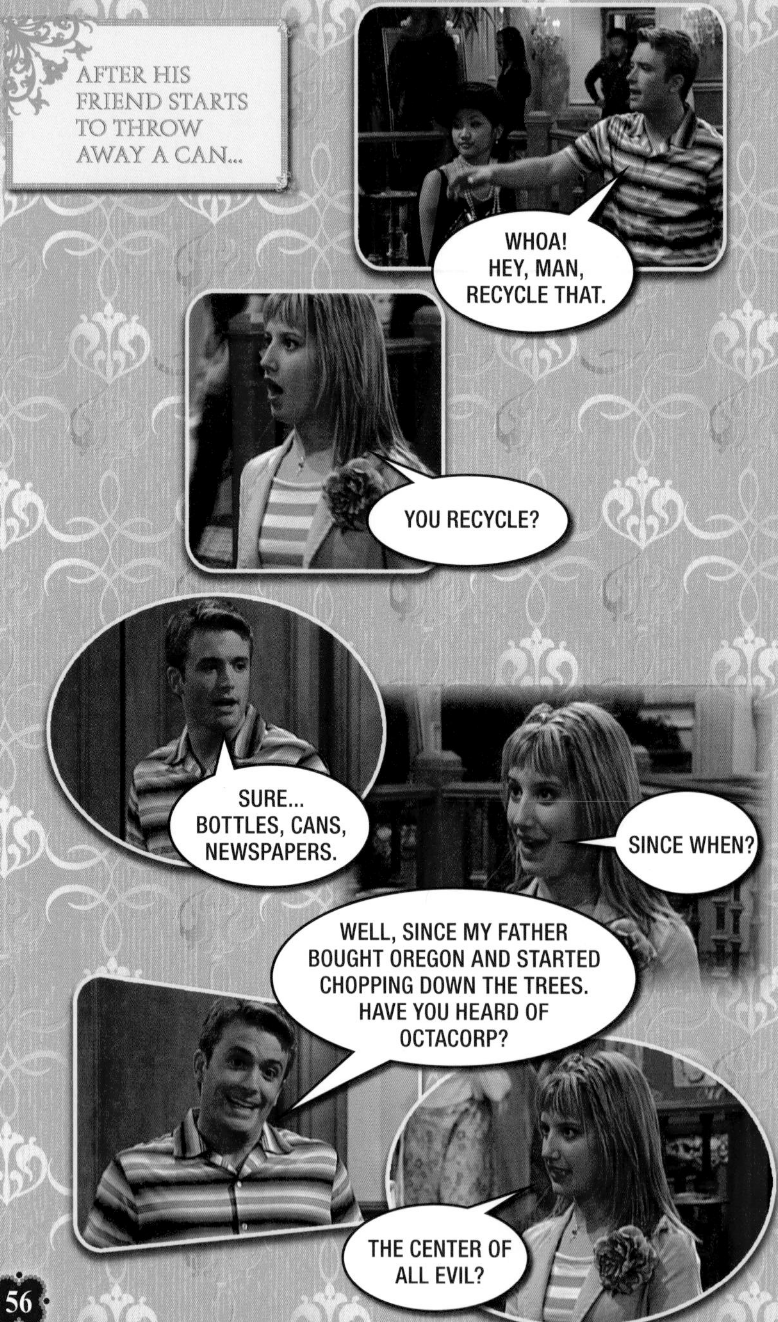
AFTER HIS FRIEND STARTS TO THROW AWAY A CAN...
WHOA! HEY, MAN, RECYCLE THAT.
YOU RECYCLE?
SURE... BOTTLES, CANS, NEWSPAPERS.
SINCE WHEN?
WELL, SINCE MY FATHER BOUGHT OREGON AND STARTED CHOPPING DOWN THE TREES. HAVE YOU HEARD OF OCTACORP?
THE CENTER OF ALL EVIL?

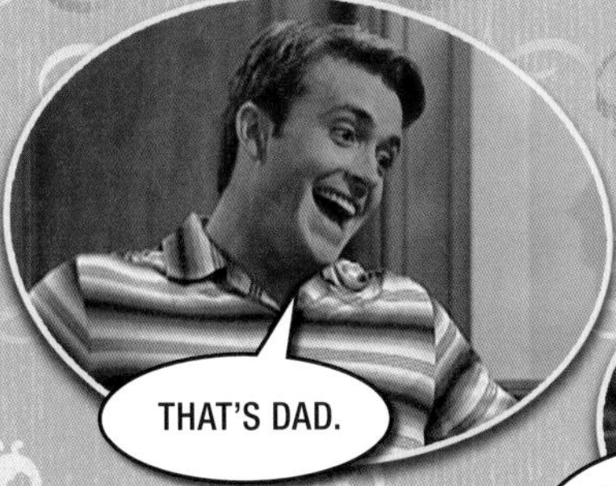
THAT'S DAD.

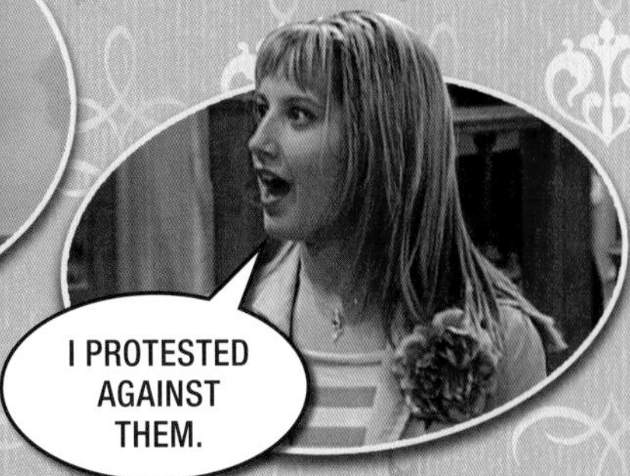
I PROTESTED AGAINST THEM.

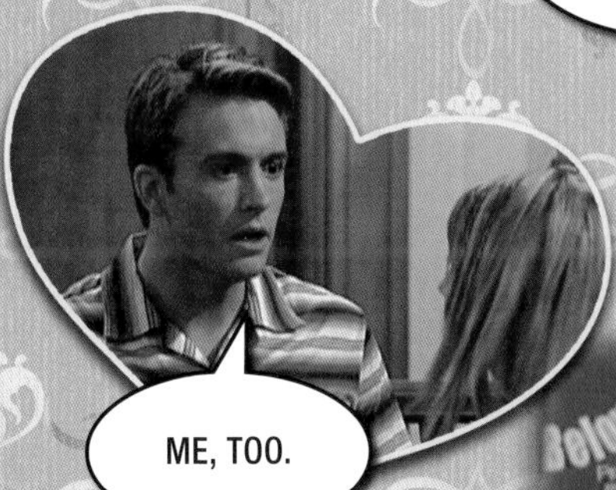
ME, TOO.

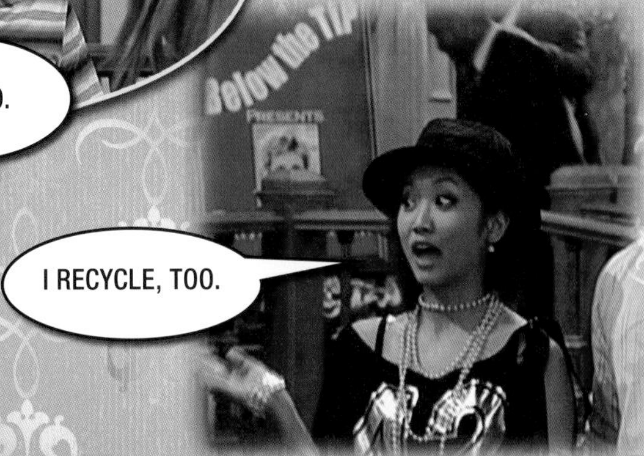
I RECYCLE, TOO.

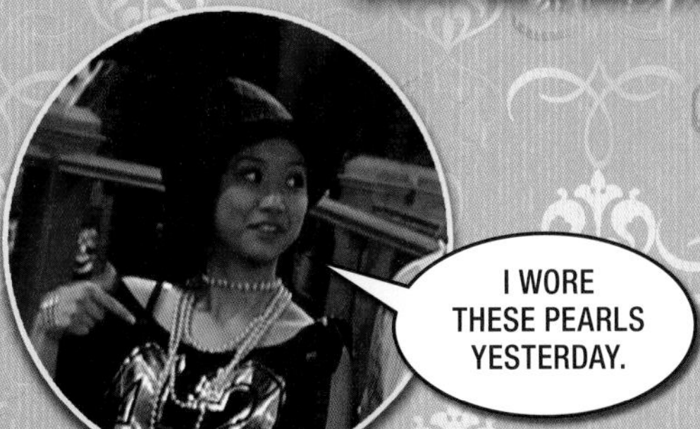
I WORE THESE PEARLS YESTERDAY.

THE NEXT MORNING...

OH, KYLE! JASON!

I GOT US TICKETS TO SEE USHER. FRONT ROW. SO CLOSE HE'LL PROBABLY SWEAT ON US.

THEN MADDIE ENTERS FOR WORK, STILL IN HER STREET CLOTHES...

EXCUSE ME. HEY, MADDIE.
WHAT IS THAT ALL ABOUT?

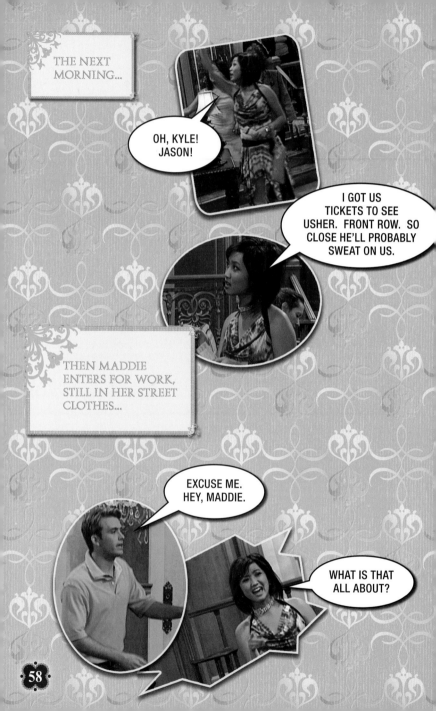

KYLE TELLS LONDON THAT MADDIE IS ALL JASON COULD TALK ABOUT LAST NIGHT... AND THAT JASON THINKS MADDIE IS RICH.

WHAT? HE THOUGHT— HA! I DON'T WANT TO BURST ANY BUBBLES... BUT IT'S SO MUCH FUN!

LONDON, A WORD.

I COULDN'T HELP OVERHEARING YOUR PLANS—

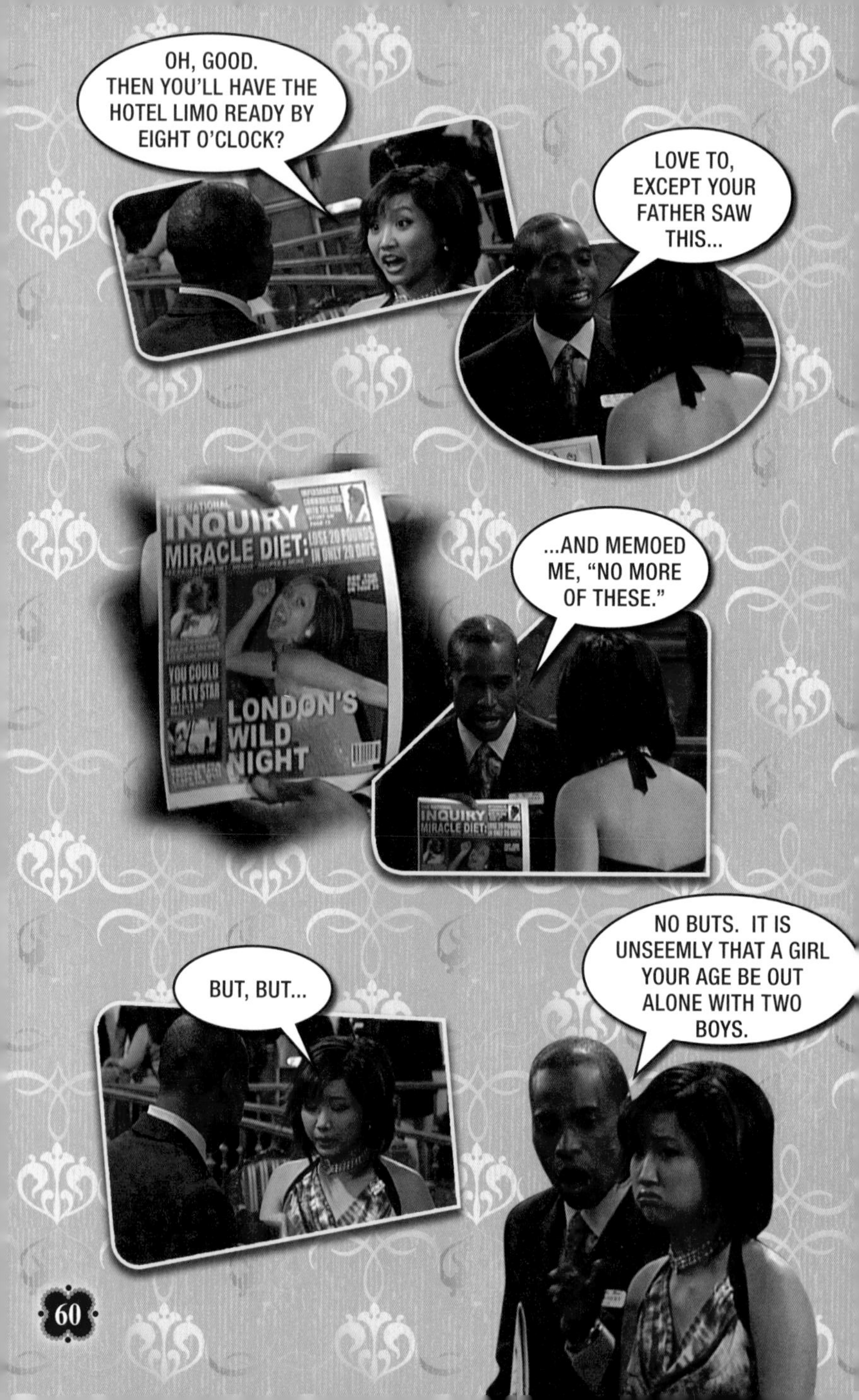
OH, GOOD. THEN YOU'LL HAVE THE HOTEL LIMO READY BY EIGHT O'CLOCK?
LOVE TO, EXCEPT YOUR FATHER SAW THIS...
THE NATIONAL INQUIRY
MIRACLE DIET: LOSE 20 POUNDS IN ONLY 20 DAYS
YOU COULD BE A TV STAR
LONDON'S WILD NIGHT
...AND MEMOED ME, "NO MORE OF THESE."
BUT, BUT...
NO BUTS. IT IS UNSEEMLY THAT A GIRL YOUR AGE BE OUT ALONE WITH TWO BOYS.

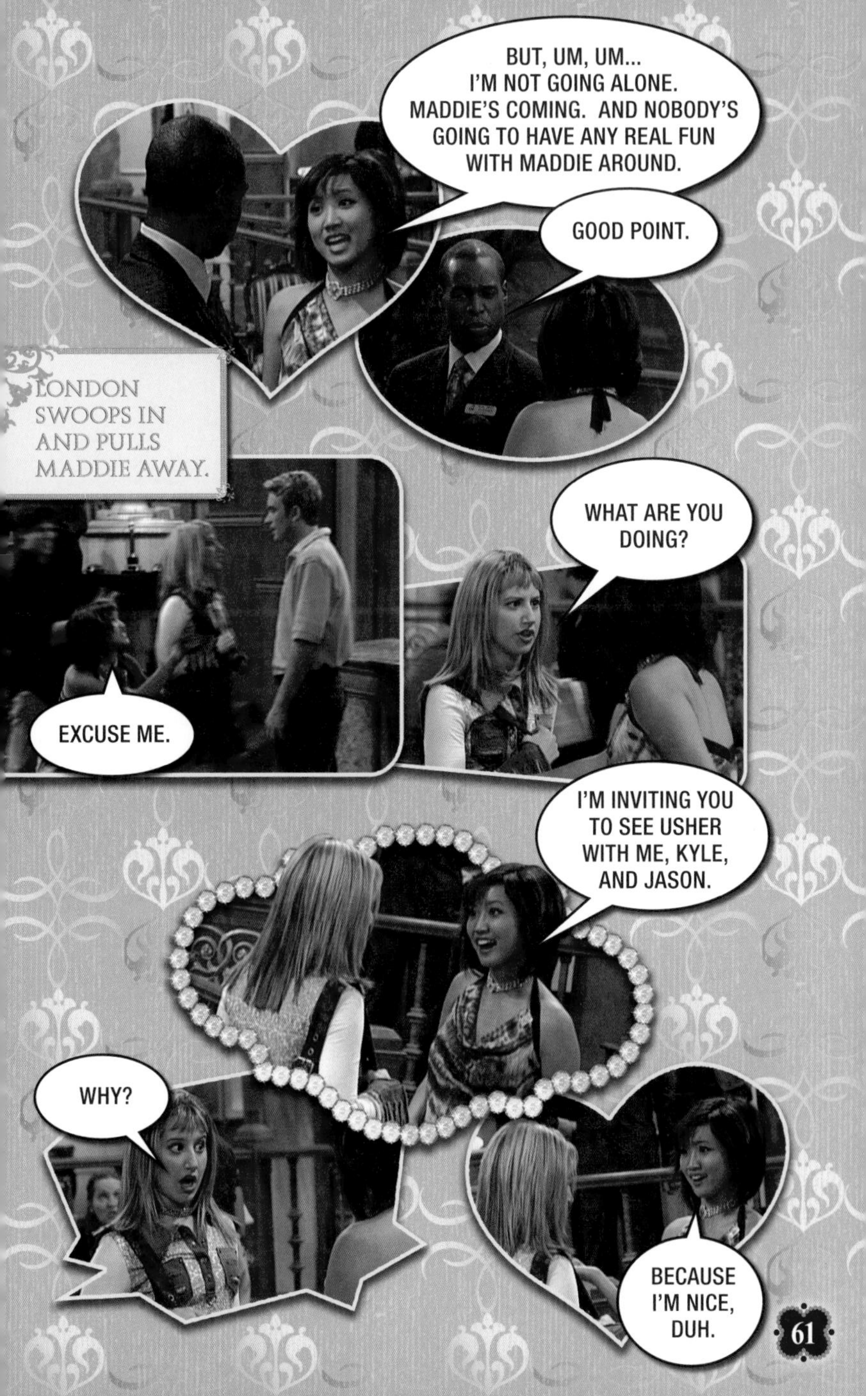
BUT, UM, UM... I'M NOT GOING ALONE. MADDIE'S COMING. AND NOBODY'S GOING TO HAVE ANY REAL FUN WITH MADDIE AROUND.
GOOD POINT.
LONDON SWOOPS IN AND PULLS MADDIE AWAY.
EXCUSE ME.
WHAT ARE YOU DOING?
I'M INVITING YOU TO SEE USHER WITH ME, KYLE, AND JASON.
WHY?
BECAUSE I'M NICE, DUH.

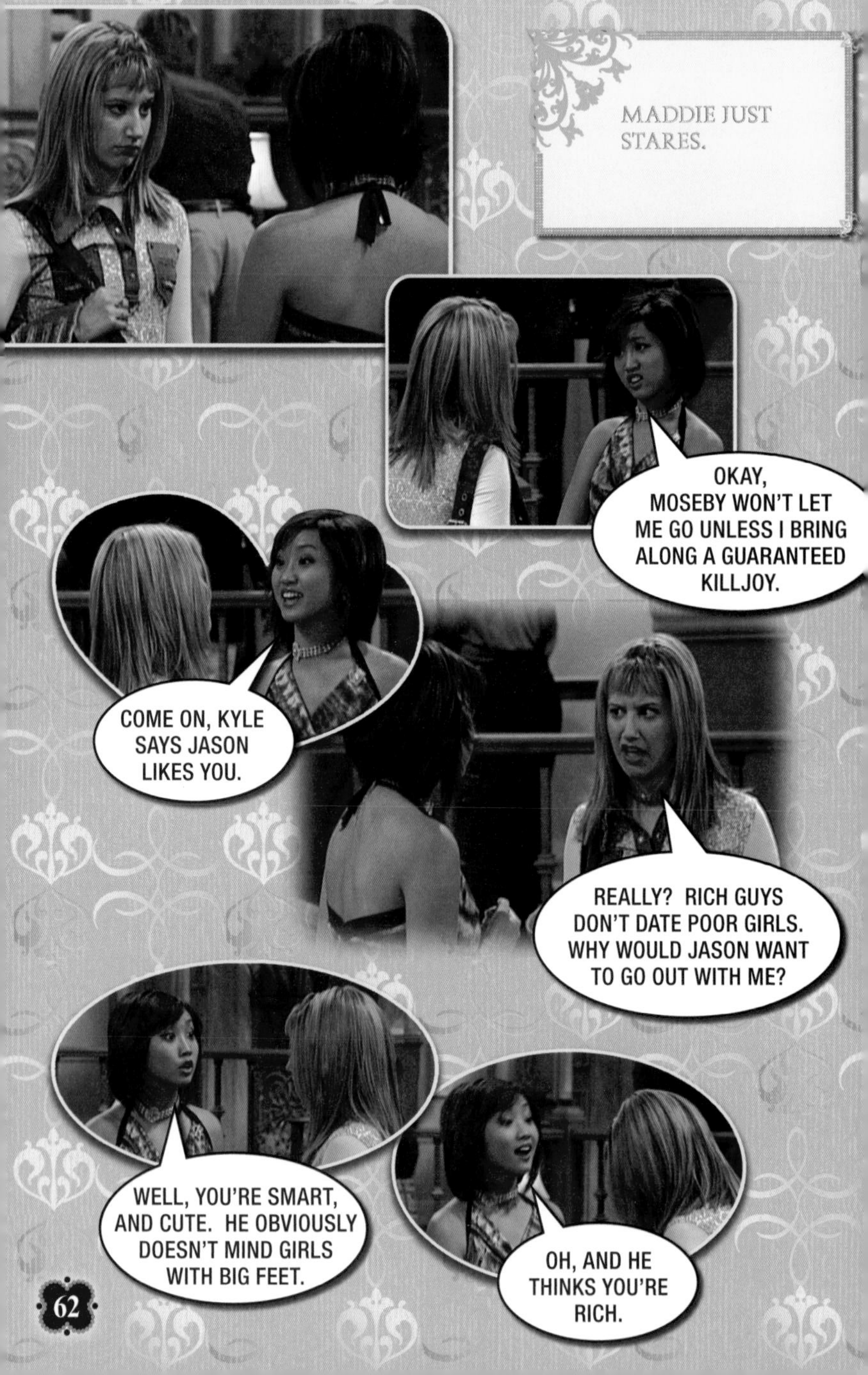
MADDIE JUST STARES.
OKAY, MOSEBY WON'T LET ME GO UNLESS I BRING ALONG A GUARANTEED KILLJOY.
COME ON, KYLE SAYS JASON LIKES YOU.
REALLY? RICH GUYS DON'T DATE POOR GIRLS. WHY WOULD JASON WANT TO GO OUT WITH ME?
WELL, YOU'RE SMART, AND CUTE. HE OBVIOUSLY DOESN'T MIND GIRLS WITH BIG FEET.
OH, AND HE THINKS YOU'RE RICH.

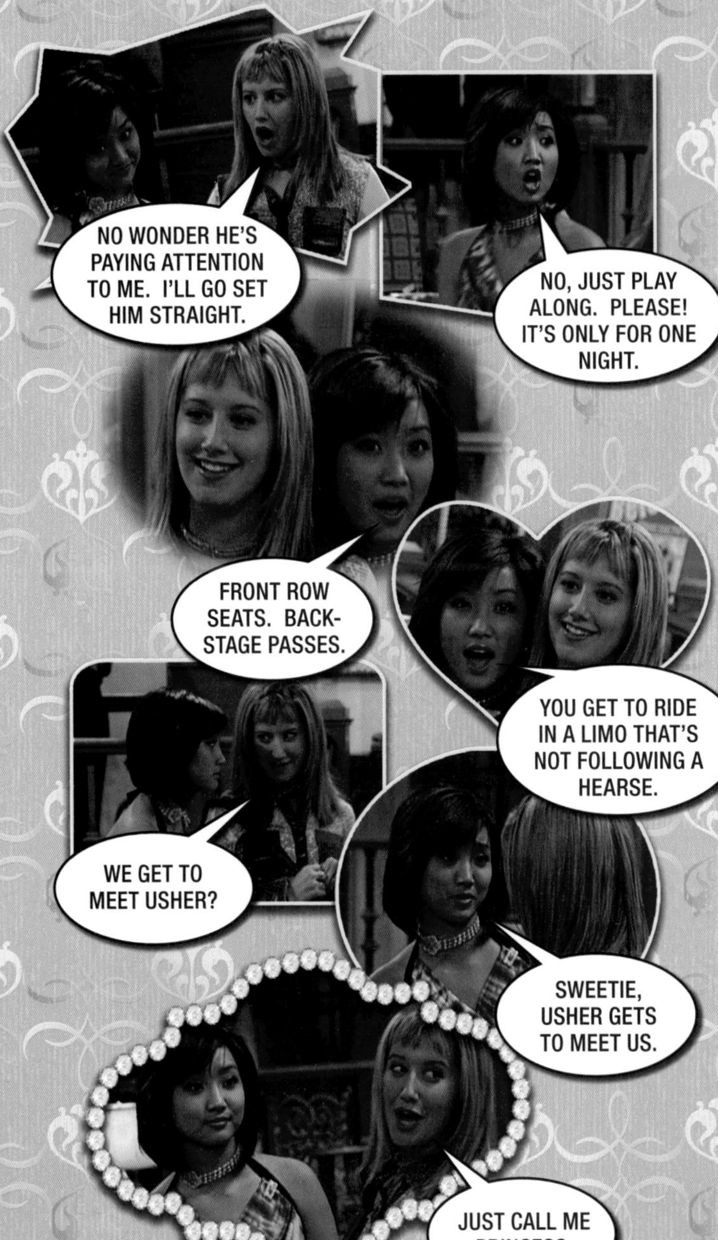
NO WONDER HE'S PAYING ATTENTION TO ME. I'LL GO SET HIM STRAIGHT.
NO, JUST PLAY ALONG. PLEASE! IT'S ONLY FOR ONE NIGHT.
FRONT ROW SEATS. BACK-STAGE PASSES.
YOU GET TO RIDE IN A LIMO THAT'S NOT FOLLOWING A HEARSE.
WE GET TO MEET USHER?
SWEETIE, USHER GETS TO MEET US.
JUST CALL ME PRINCESS.

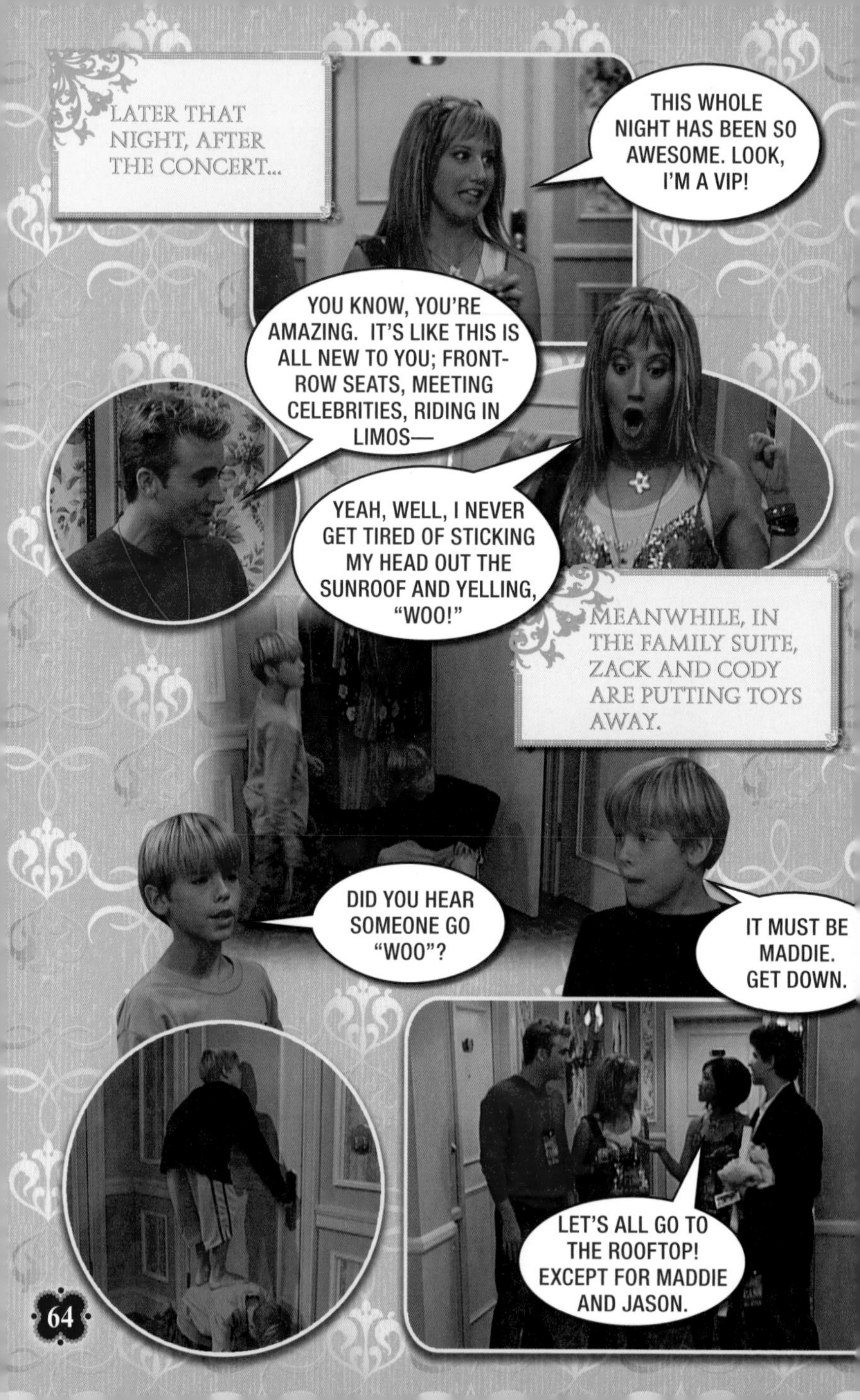
LATER THAT NIGHT, AFTER THE CONCERT...
THIS WHOLE NIGHT HAS BEEN SO AWESOME. LOOK, I'M A VIP!
YOU KNOW, YOU'RE AMAZING. IT'S LIKE THIS IS ALL NEW TO YOU; FRONT-ROW SEATS, MEETING CELEBRITIES, RIDING IN LIMOS—
YEAH, WELL, I NEVER GET TIRED OF STICKING MY HEAD OUT THE SUNROOF AND YELLING, "WOO!"
MEANWHILE, IN THE FAMILY SUITE, ZACK AND CODY ARE PUTTING TOYS AWAY.
DID YOU HEAR SOMEONE GO "WOO"?
IT MUST BE MADDIE. GET DOWN.
LET'S ALL GO TO THE ROOFTOP! EXCEPT FOR MADDIE AND JASON.

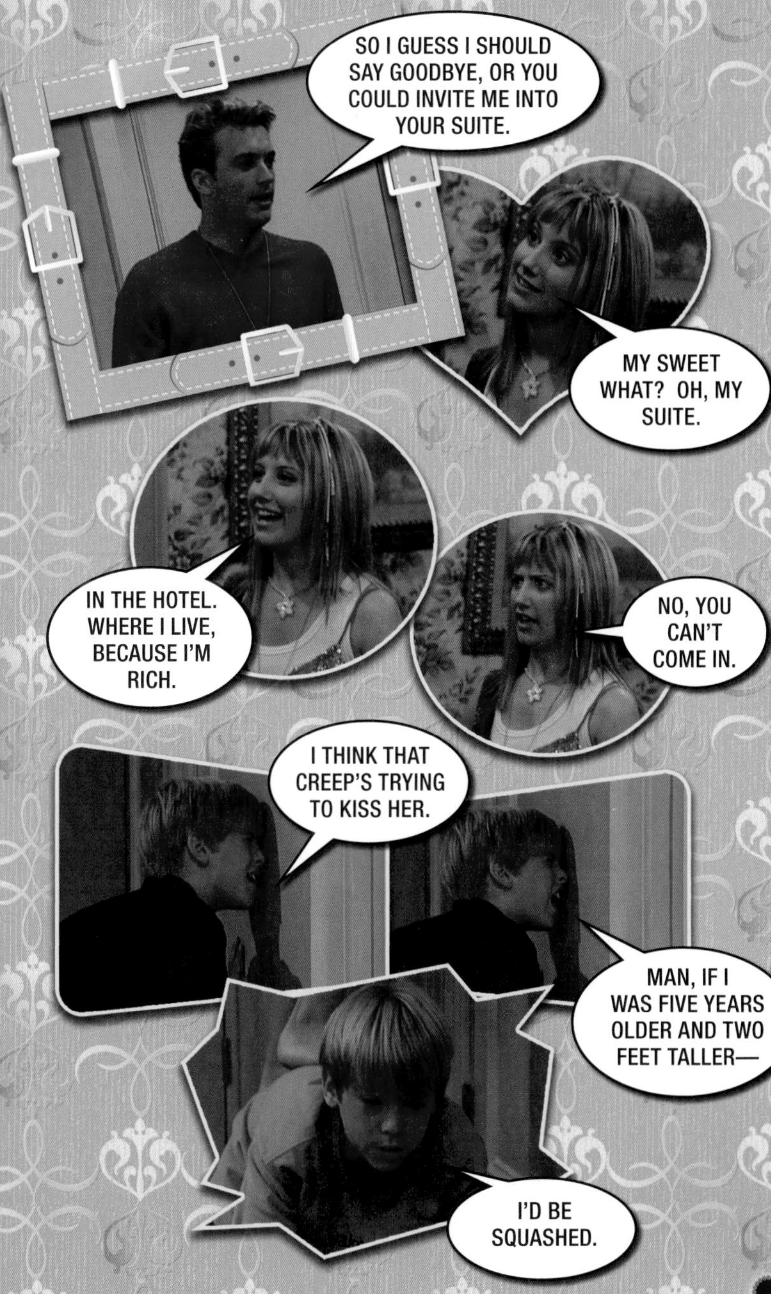
SO I GUESS I SHOULD SAY GOODBYE, OR YOU COULD INVITE ME INTO YOUR SUITE.
MY SWEET WHAT? OH, MY SUITE.
IN THE HOTEL. WHERE I LIVE, BECAUSE I'M RICH.
NO, YOU CAN'T COME IN.
I THINK THAT CREEP'S TRYING TO KISS HER.
MAN, IF I WAS FIVE YEARS OLDER AND TWO FEET TALLER—
I'D BE SQUASHED.

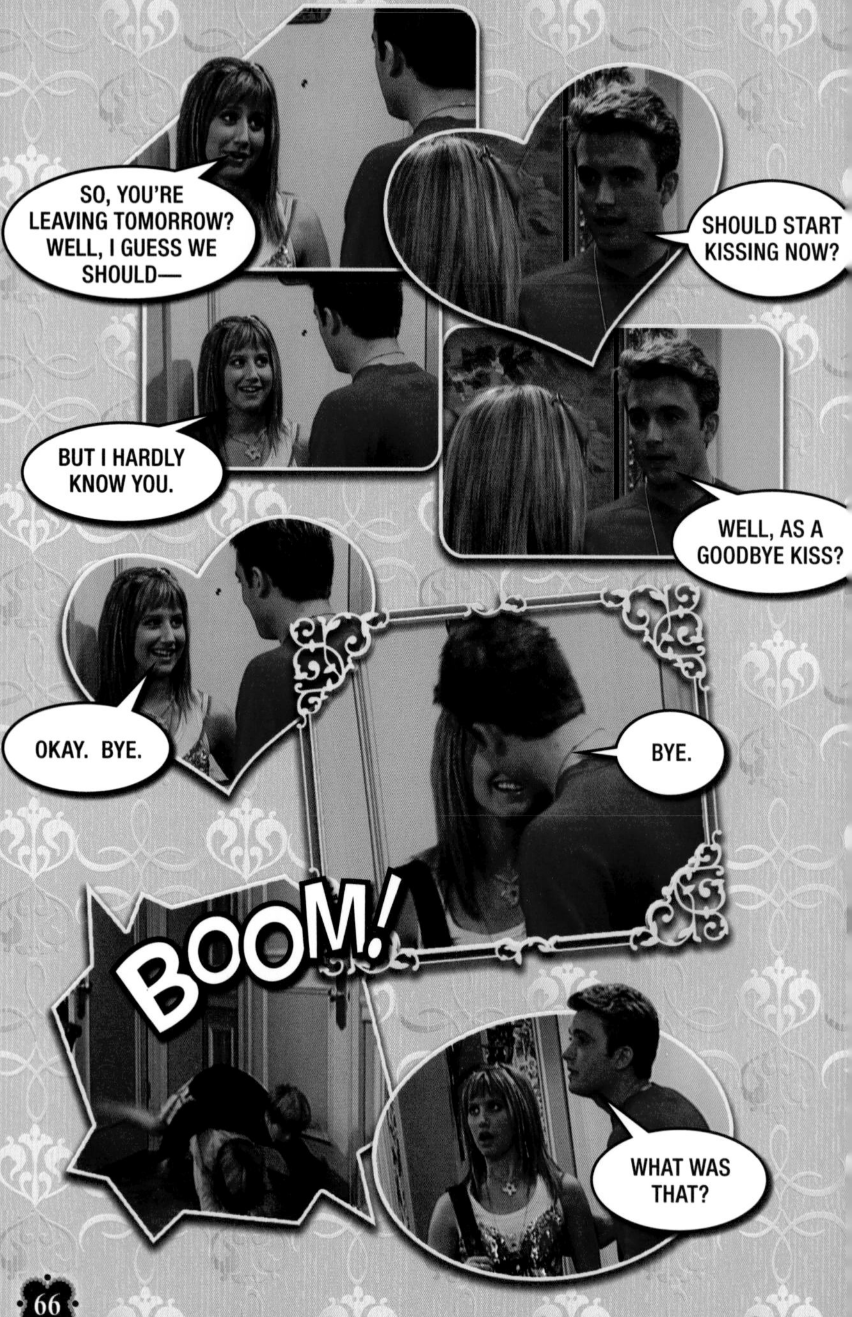
SO, YOU'RE LEAVING TOMORROW? WELL, I GUESS WE SHOULD—
SHOULD START KISSING NOW?
BUT I HARDLY KNOW YOU.
WELL, AS A GOODBYE KISS?
OKAY. BYE.
BYE.
BOOM!
WHAT WAS THAT?

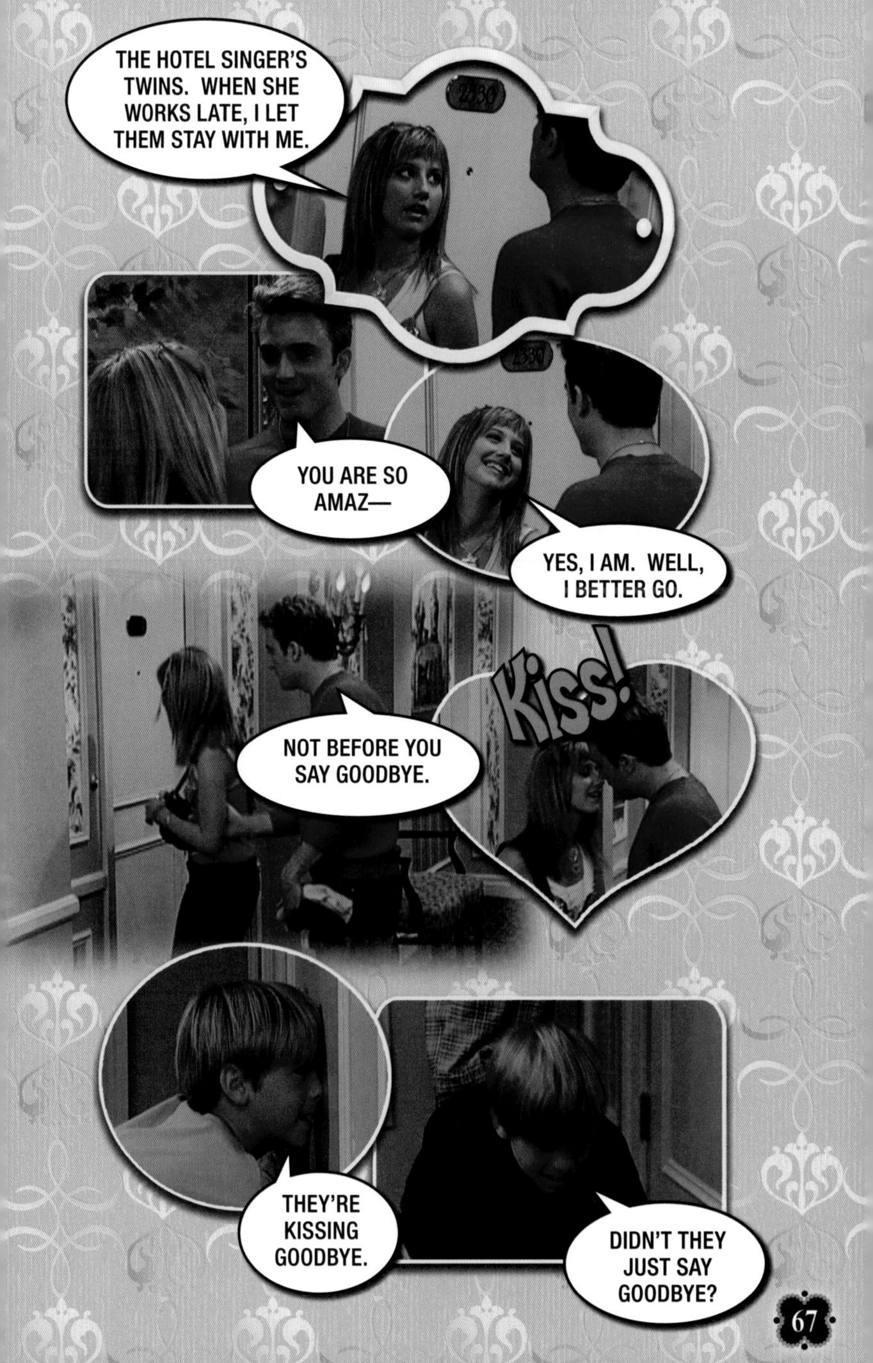
THE HOTEL SINGER'S TWINS. WHEN SHE WORKS LATE, I LET THEM STAY WITH ME.
YOU ARE SO AMAZ—
YES, I AM. WELL, I BETTER GO.
NOT BEFORE YOU SAY GOODBYE.
Kiss!
THEY'RE KISSING GOODBYE.
DIDN'T THEY JUST SAY GOODBYE?

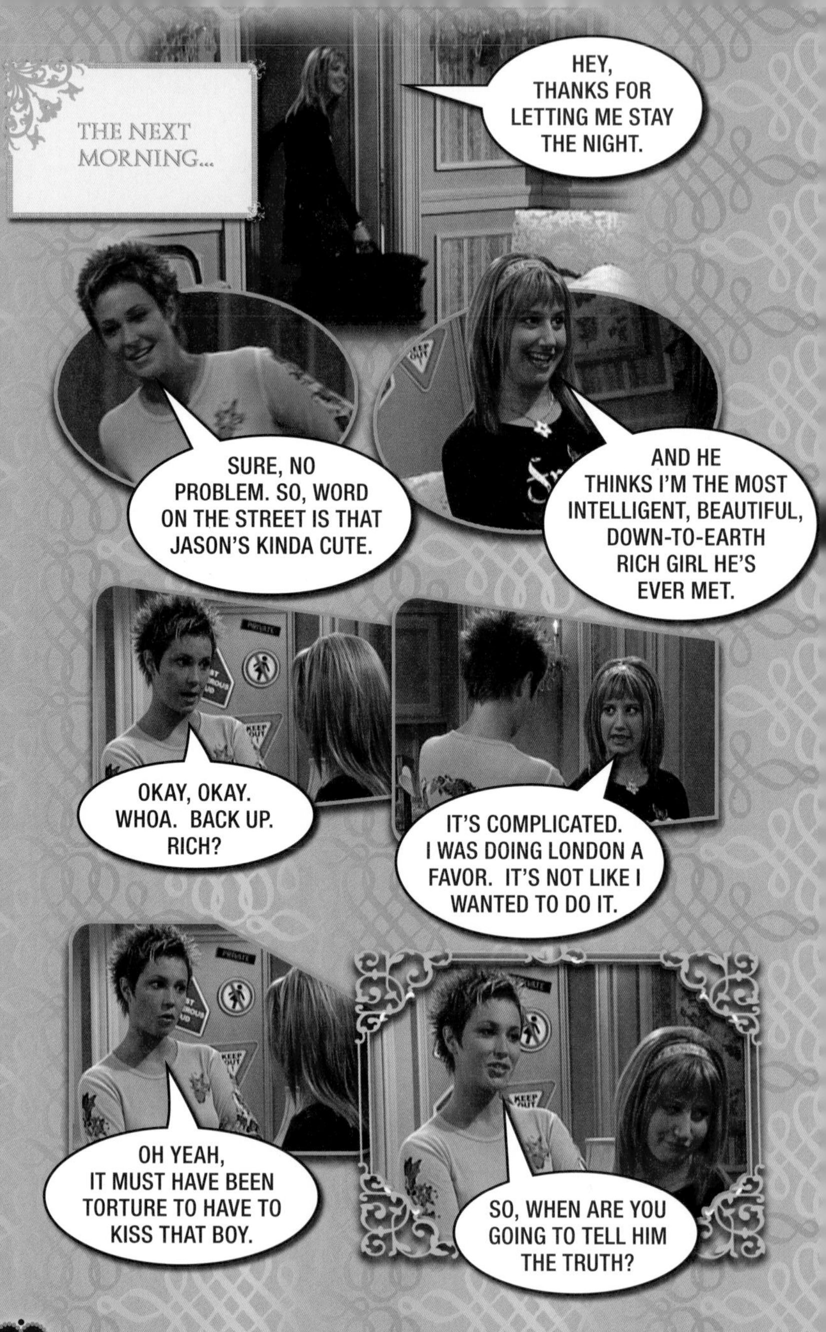
THE NEXT MORNING...
HEY, THANKS FOR LETTING ME STAY THE NIGHT.
SURE, NO PROBLEM. SO, WORD ON THE STREET IS THAT JASON'S KINDA CUTE.
AND HE THINKS I'M THE MOST INTELLIGENT, BEAUTIFUL, DOWN-TO-EARTH RICH GIRL HE'S EVER MET.
OKAY, OKAY. WHOA. BACK UP. RICH?
IT'S COMPLICATED. I WAS DOING LONDON A FAVOR. IT'S NOT LIKE I WANTED TO DO IT.
OH YEAH, IT MUST HAVE BEEN TORTURE TO HAVE TO KISS THAT BOY.
SO, WHEN ARE YOU GOING TO TELL HIM THE TRUTH?

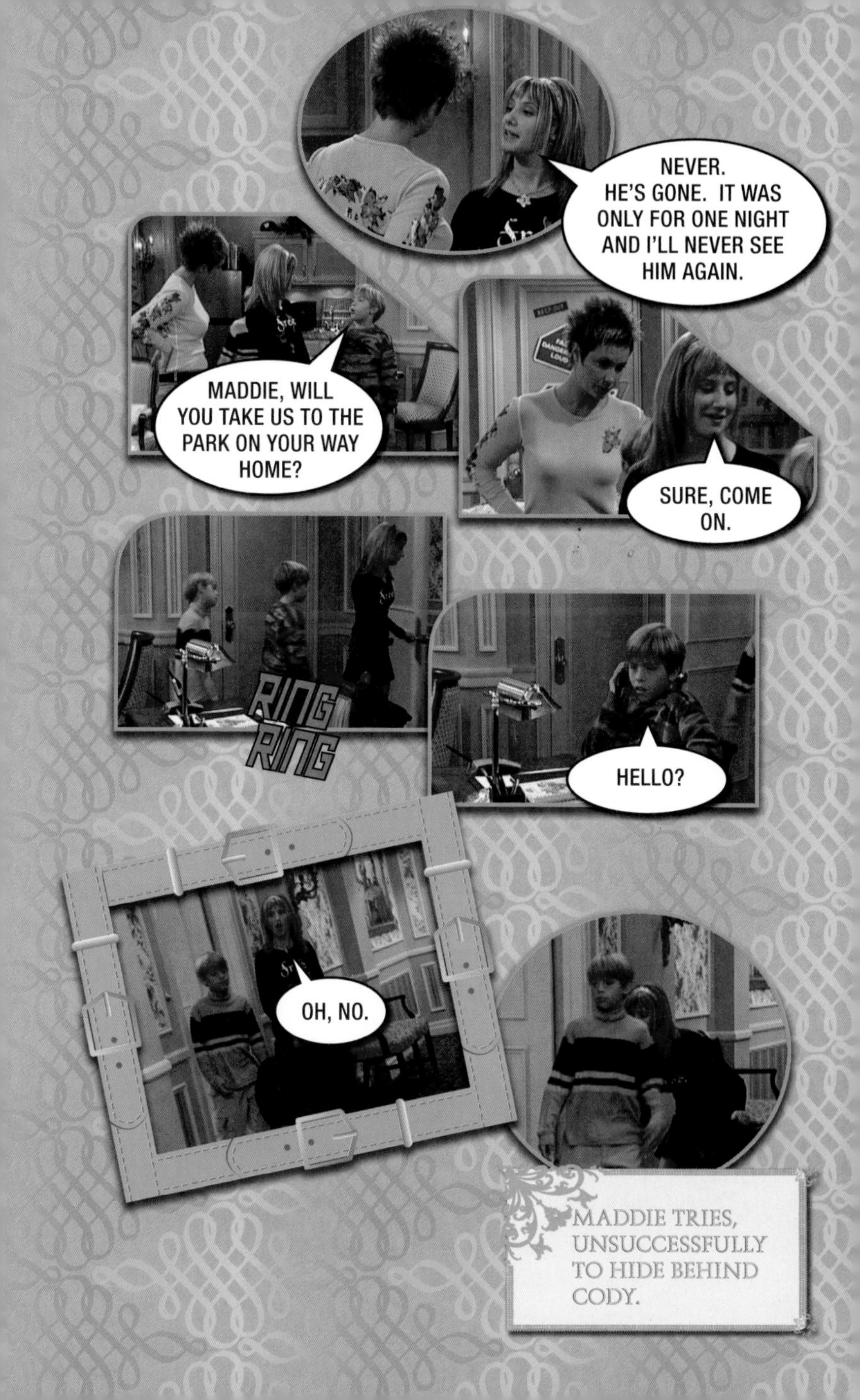
NEVER. HE'S GONE. IT WAS ONLY FOR ONE NIGHT AND I'LL NEVER SEE HIM AGAIN.
MADDIE, WILL YOU TAKE US TO THE PARK ON YOUR WAY HOME?
SURE, COME ON.
RING RING
HELLO?
OH, NO.
MADDIE TRIES, UNSUCCESSFULLY TO HIDE BEHIND CODY.

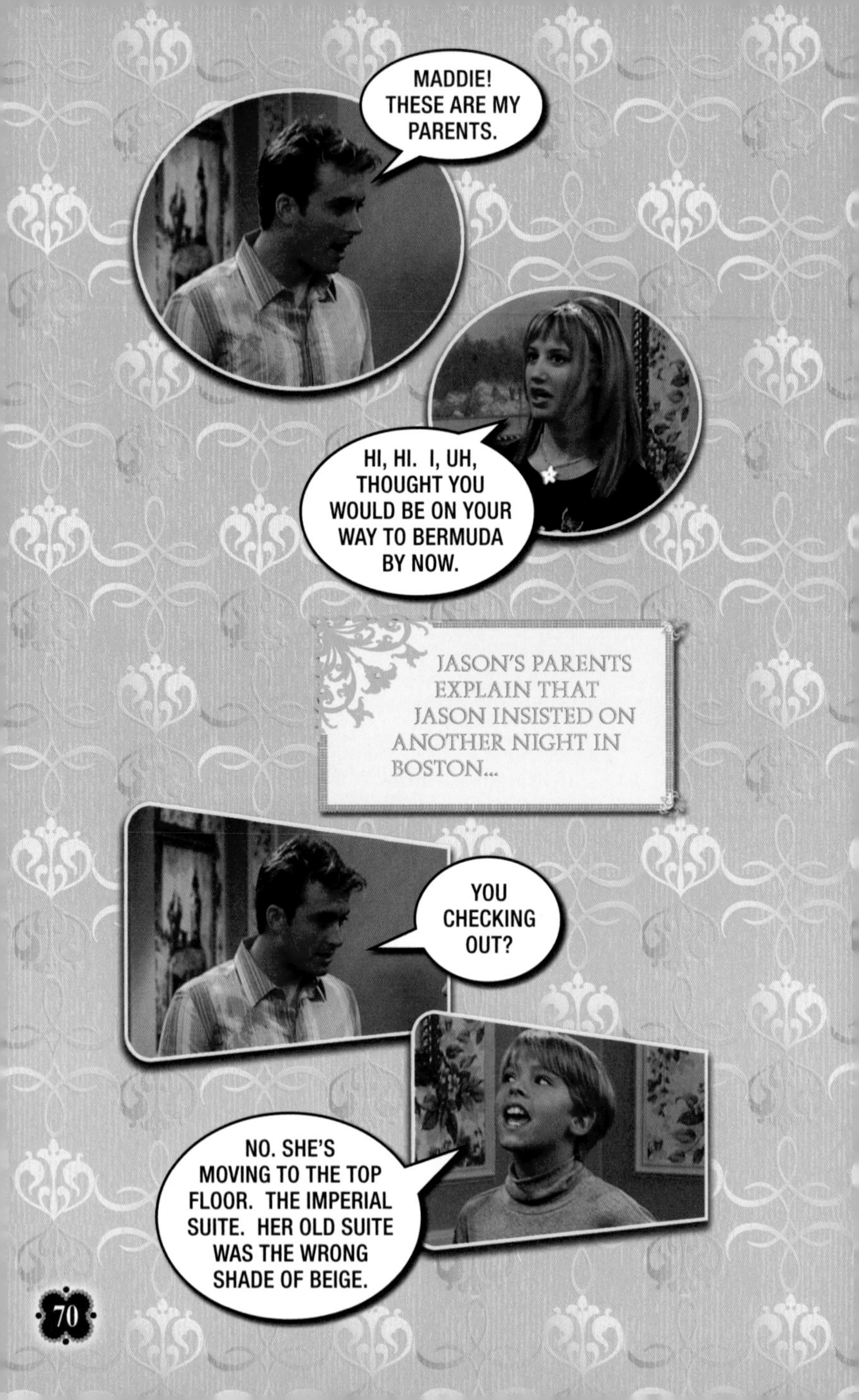
MADDIE! THESE ARE MY PARENTS.
HI, HI. I, UH, THOUGHT YOU WOULD BE ON YOUR WAY TO BERMUDA BY NOW.
JASON'S PARENTS EXPLAIN THAT JASON INSISTED ON ANOTHER NIGHT IN BOSTON...
YOU CHECKING OUT?
NO. SHE'S MOVING TO THE TOP FLOOR. THE IMPERIAL SUITE. HER OLD SUITE WAS THE WRONG SHADE OF BEIGE.

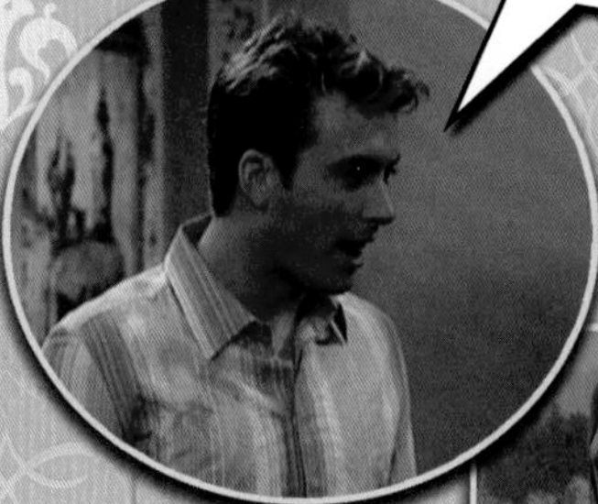
WELL, WE WERE JUST COMING DOWN TO INVITE YOU TO DINNER. I CONVINCED MY PARENTS TO TAKE US TO CLUB NOUVEAU.

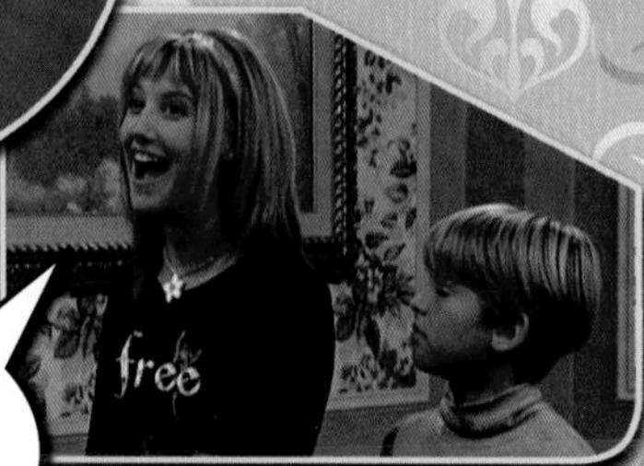
free
REALLY? WOW... I CAN'T GO. YEAH, I PROMISED I'D BABYSIT THE BOYS TONIGHT.

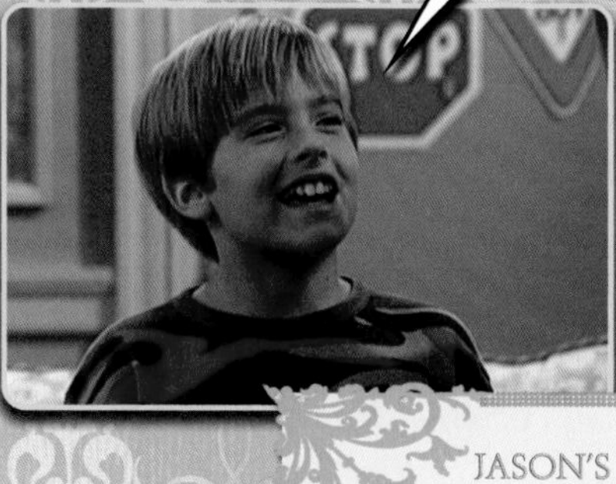
CODY, HEY, JOSH CALLED. WE'RE SLEEPING OVER AT HIS HOUSE TONIGHT.
STOP

JASON'S DAD INSISTS THAT MADDIE JOIN THEM. HE TELLS MADDIE THEY'LL PICK HER UP AT SEVEN O'CLOCK SHARP.

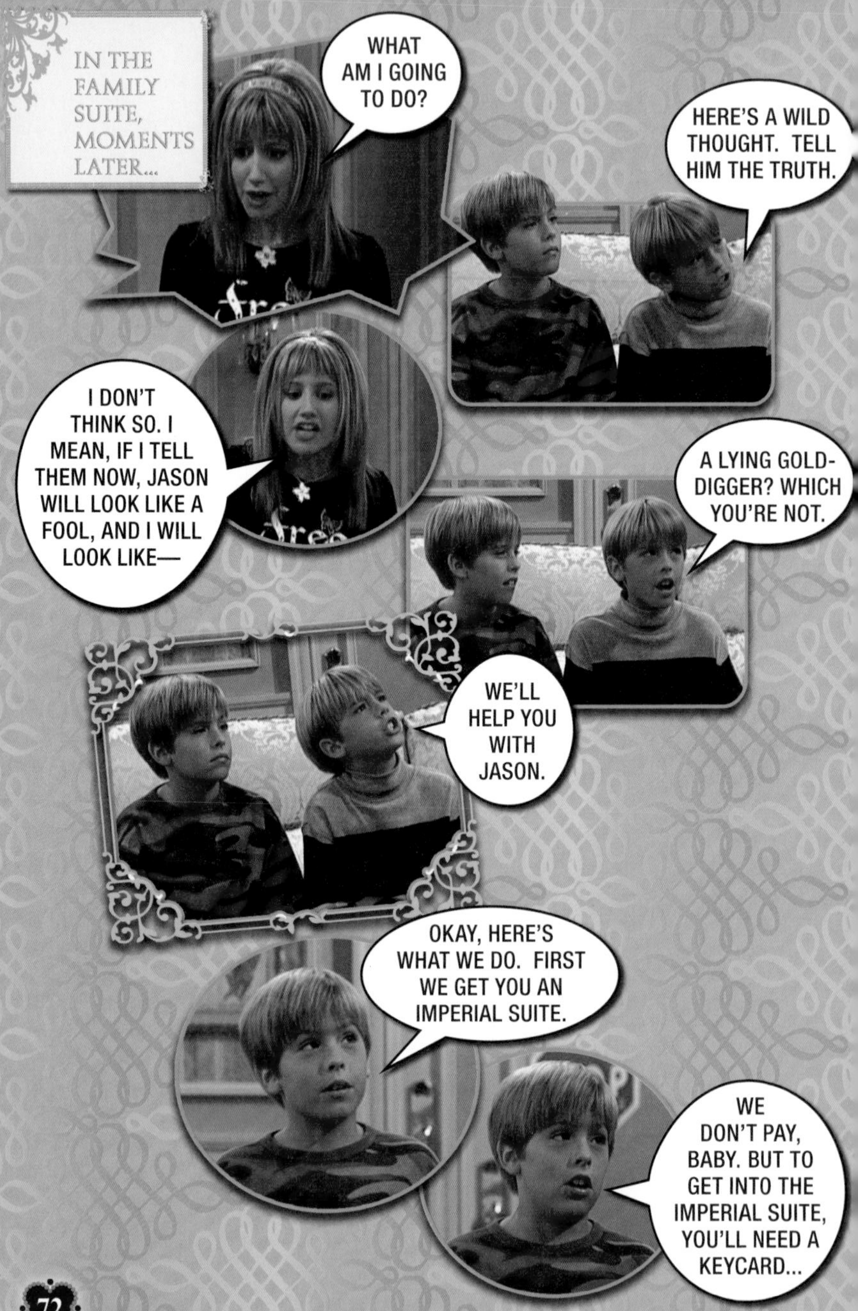
IN THE FAMILY SUITE, MOMENTS LATER...
WHAT AM I GOING TO DO?
HERE'S A WILD THOUGHT. TELL HIM THE TRUTH.
I DON'T THINK SO. I MEAN, IF I TELL THEM NOW, JASON WILL LOOK LIKE A FOOL, AND I WILL LOOK LIKE—
A LYING GOLD-DIGGER? WHICH YOU'RE NOT.
WE'LL HELP YOU WITH JASON.
OKAY, HERE'S WHAT WE DO. FIRST WE GET YOU AN IMPERIAL SUITE.
WE DON'T PAY, BABY. BUT TO GET INTO THE IMPERIAL SUITE, YOU'LL NEED A KEYCARD...

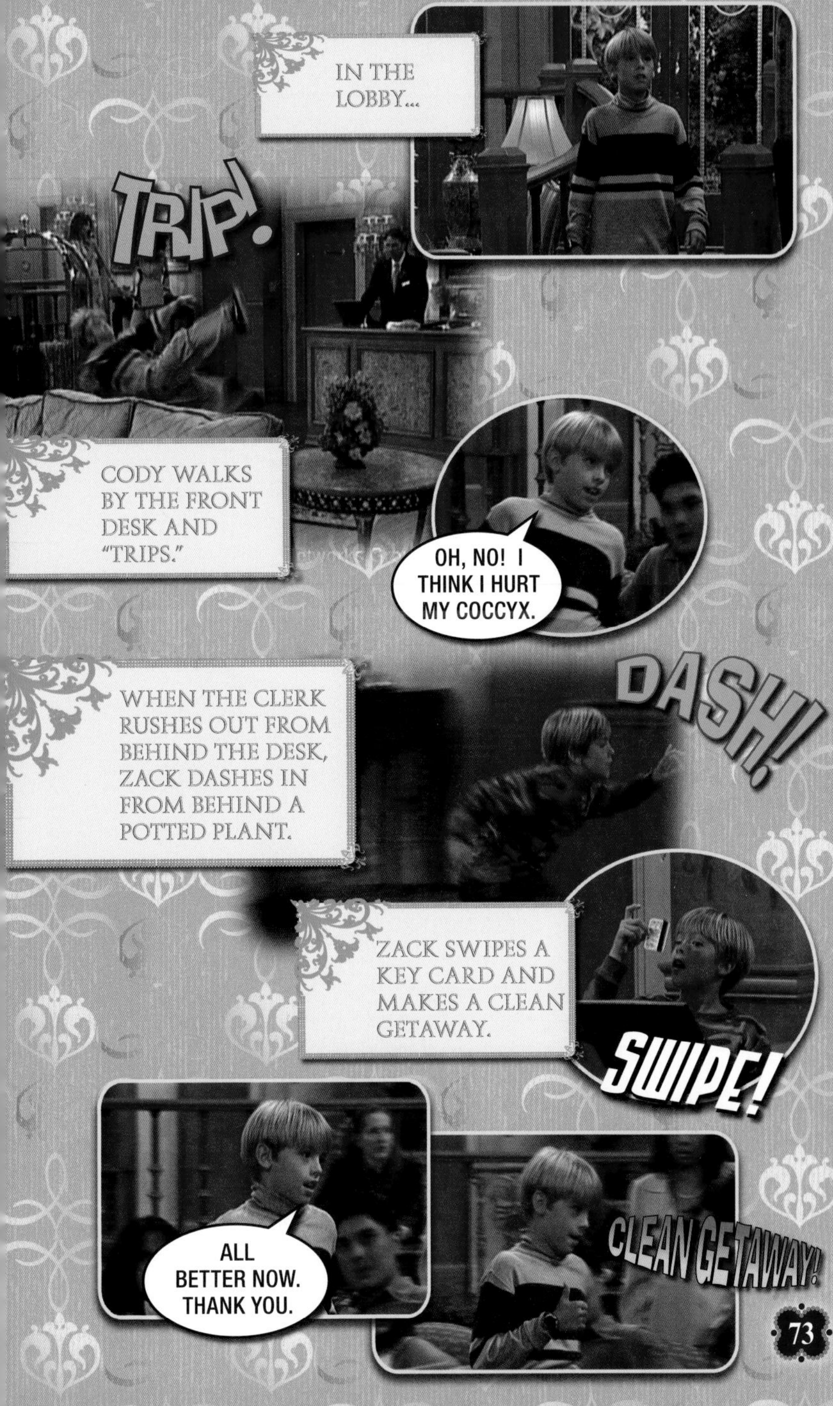
IN THE LOBBY...
TRIP!
CODY WALKS BY THE FRONT DESK AND "TRIPS."
OH, NO! I THINK I HURT MY COCCYX.
WHEN THE CLERK RUSHES OUT FROM BEHIND THE DESK, ZACK DASHES IN FROM BEHIND A POTTED PLANT.
DASH!
ZACK SWIPES A KEY CARD AND MAKES A CLEAN GETAWAY.
SWIPE!
ALL BETTER NOW. THANK YOU.
CLEAN GETAWAY!

WHEN MADDIE TELLS THE TWINS SHE DOESN'T HAVE ANYTHING TO WEAR TO CLUB NOUVEAU, THEY ACCEPT THE CHALLENGE.

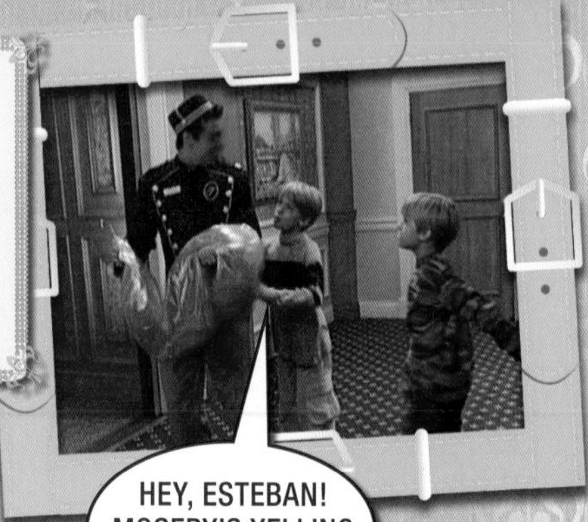
HEY, ESTEBAN! MOSEBY'S YELLING FOR YOU.

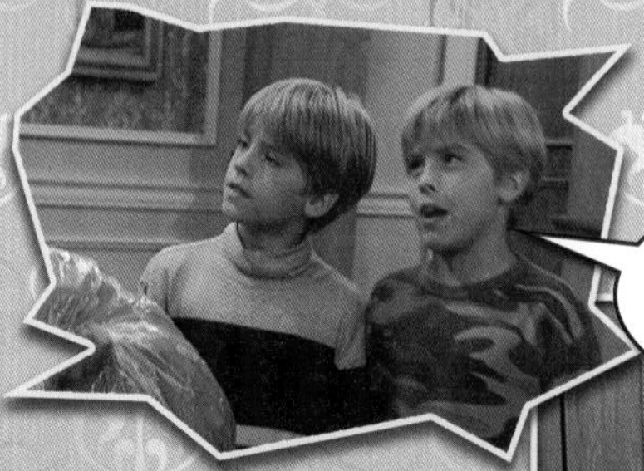
WELL, YOU'RE KEEPING A GREAT MAN WAITING.

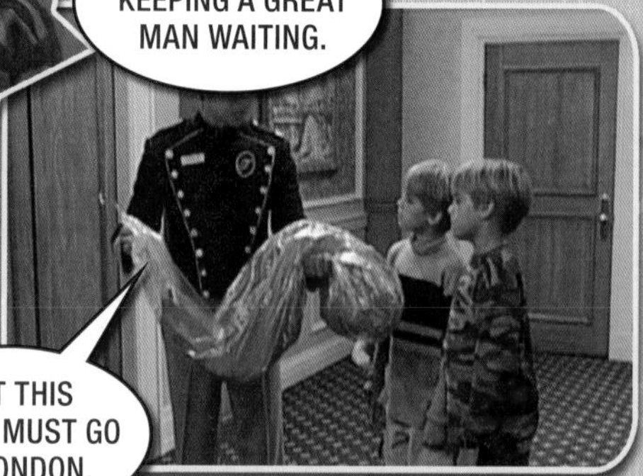
BUT THIS DRESS MUST GO TO LONDON.

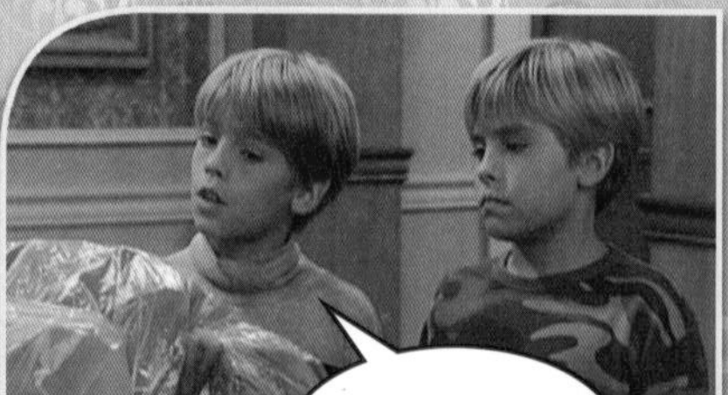
WE'LL TAKE IT.

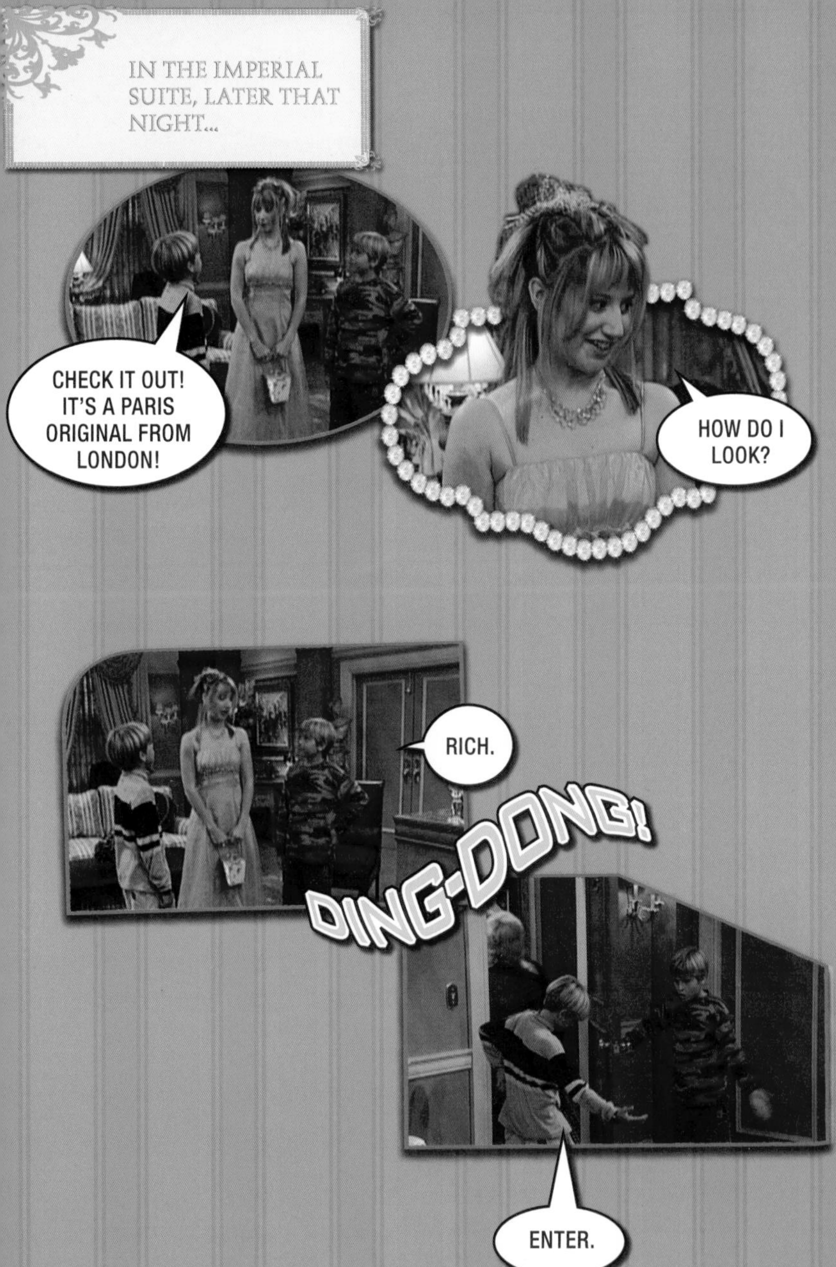
IN THE IMPERIAL SUITE, LATER THAT NIGHT...
CHECK IT OUT! IT'S A PARIS ORIGINAL FROM LONDON!
HOW DO I LOOK?
RICH.
DING-DONG!
ENTER.

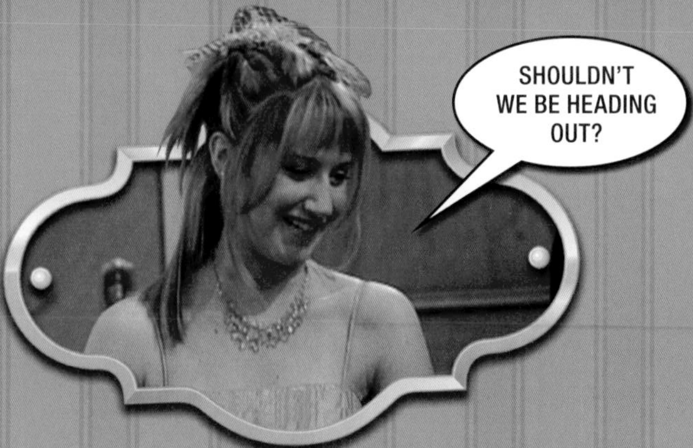
SHOULDN'T WE BE HEADING OUT?

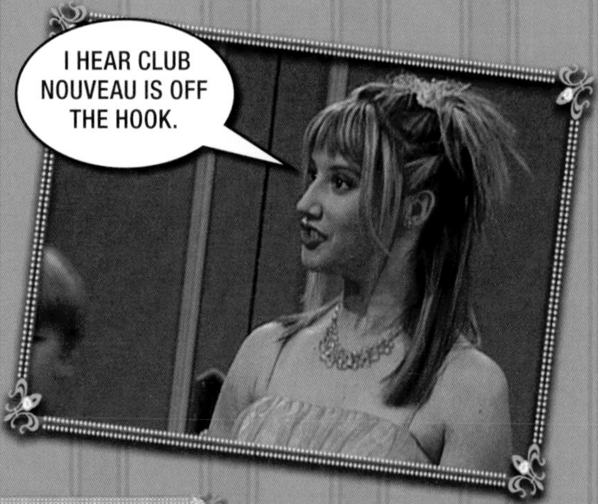
I HEAR CLUB NOUVEAU IS OFF THE HOOK.

TO MADDIE'S DISMAY, JASON'S MOM TELLS HER THE HOTTEST TICKET IN TOWN RIGHT NOW IS CAREY MARTIN... ZACK AND CODY'S MOTHER!

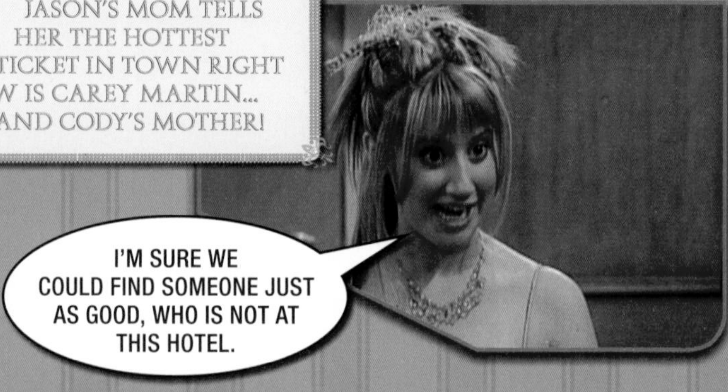
I'M SURE WE COULD FIND SOMEONE JUST AS GOOD, WHO IS NOT AT THIS HOTEL.

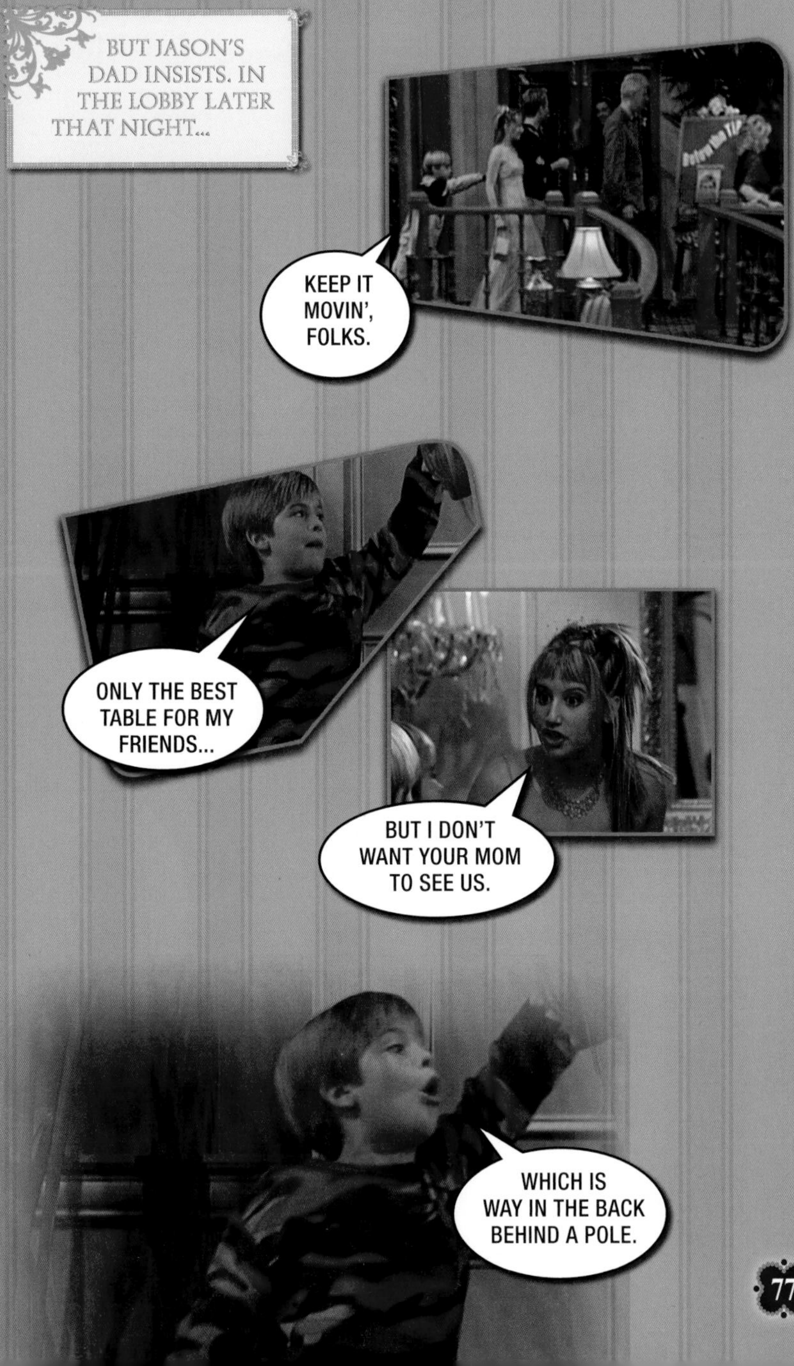
BUT JASON'S DAD INSISTS. IN THE LOBBY LATER THAT NIGHT...
KEEP IT MOVIN', FOLKS.
ONLY THE BEST TABLE FOR MY FRIENDS...
BUT I DON'T WANT YOUR MOM TO SEE US.
WHICH IS WAY IN THE BACK BEHIND A POLE.

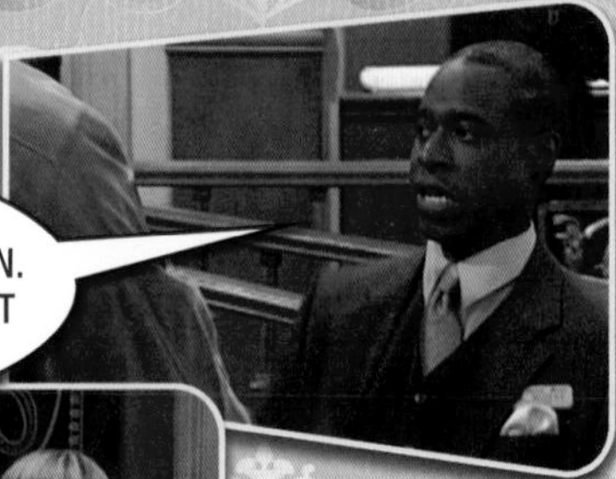
MEANWHILE, AT THE FRONT DESK...
MR. AMPUTATOR! A PLEASURE TO SEE YOU AGAIN. ANOTHER WRESTLE ROYALE AT THE GARDEN?

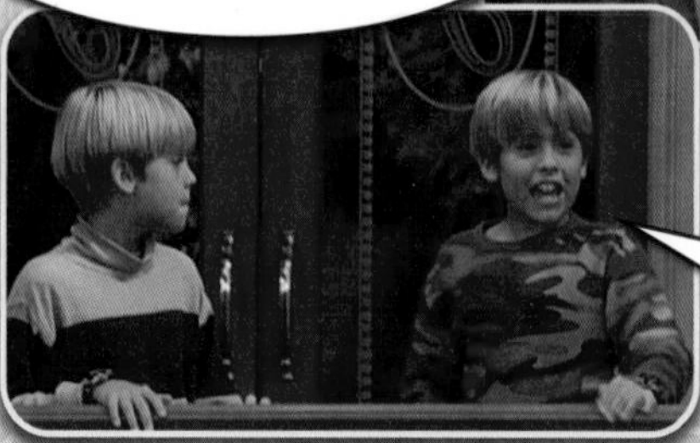
THE AMPUTATOR'S HERE! HE'S MY FAVORITE WRESTLER!

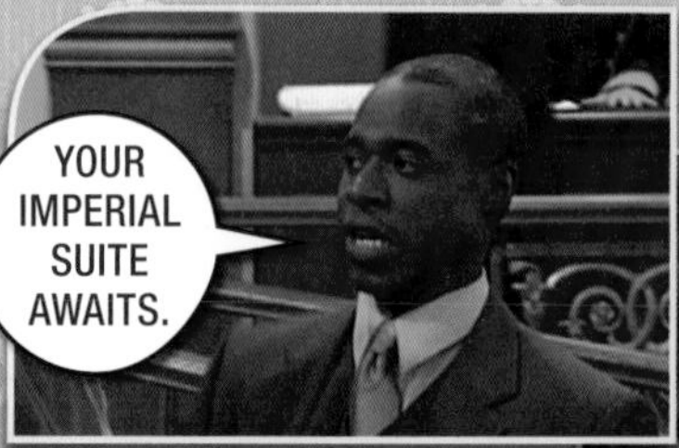
YOUR IMPERIAL SUITE AWAITS.

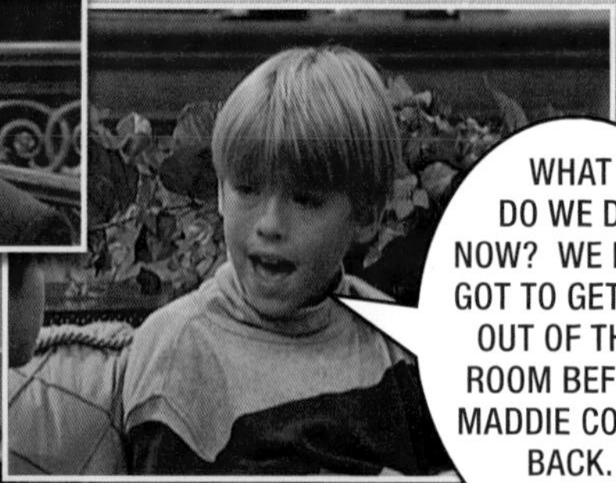
WHAT DO WE DO NOW? WE HAVE GOT TO GET HIM OUT OF THAT ROOM BEFORE MADDIE COMES BACK.

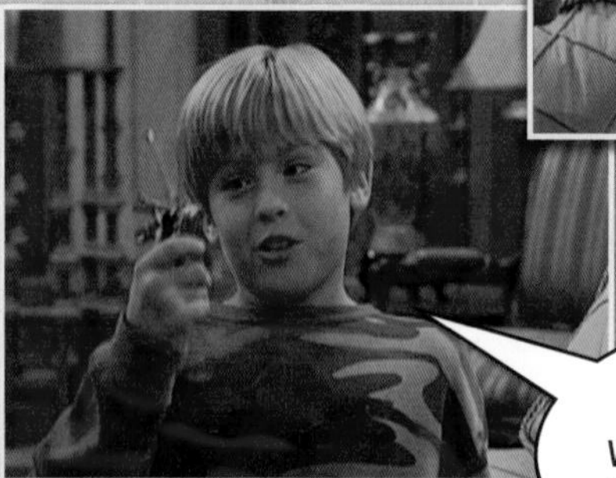
JUST STALL HIM. WHEN I'M DONE WITH THAT ROOM, HE'S GONNA WISH HE NEVER CHECKED IN.

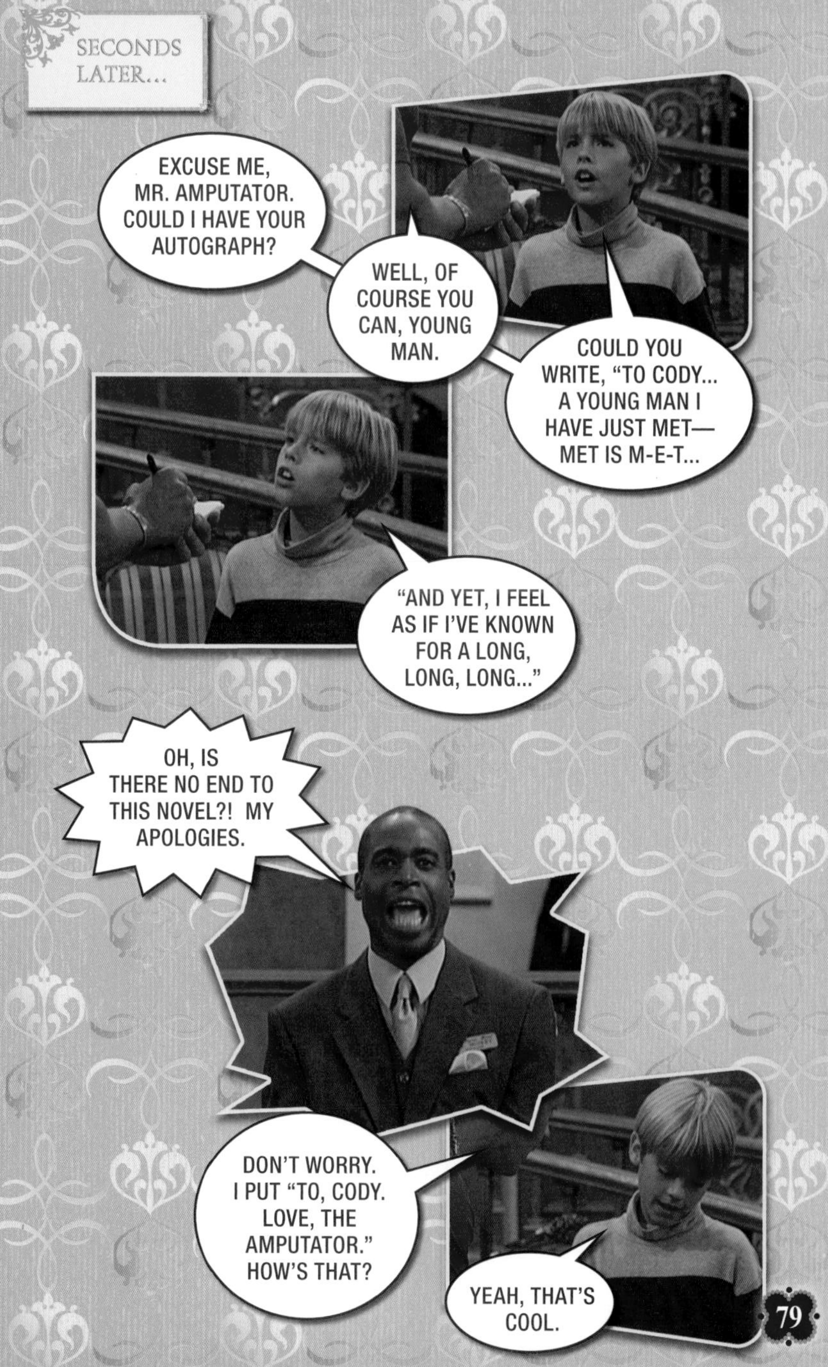
SECONDS LATER...
EXCUSE ME, MR. AMPUTATOR. COULD I HAVE YOUR AUTOGRAPH?
WELL, OF COURSE YOU CAN, YOUNG MAN.
COULD YOU WRITE, "TO CODY... A YOUNG MAN I HAVE JUST MET— MET IS M-E-T...
"AND YET, I FEEL AS IF I'VE KNOWN FOR A LONG, LONG, LONG..."
OH, IS THERE NO END TO THIS NOVEL?! MY APOLOGIES.
DON'T WORRY. I PUT "TO, CODY. LOVE, THE AMPUTATOR." HOW'S THAT?
YEAH, THAT'S COOL.

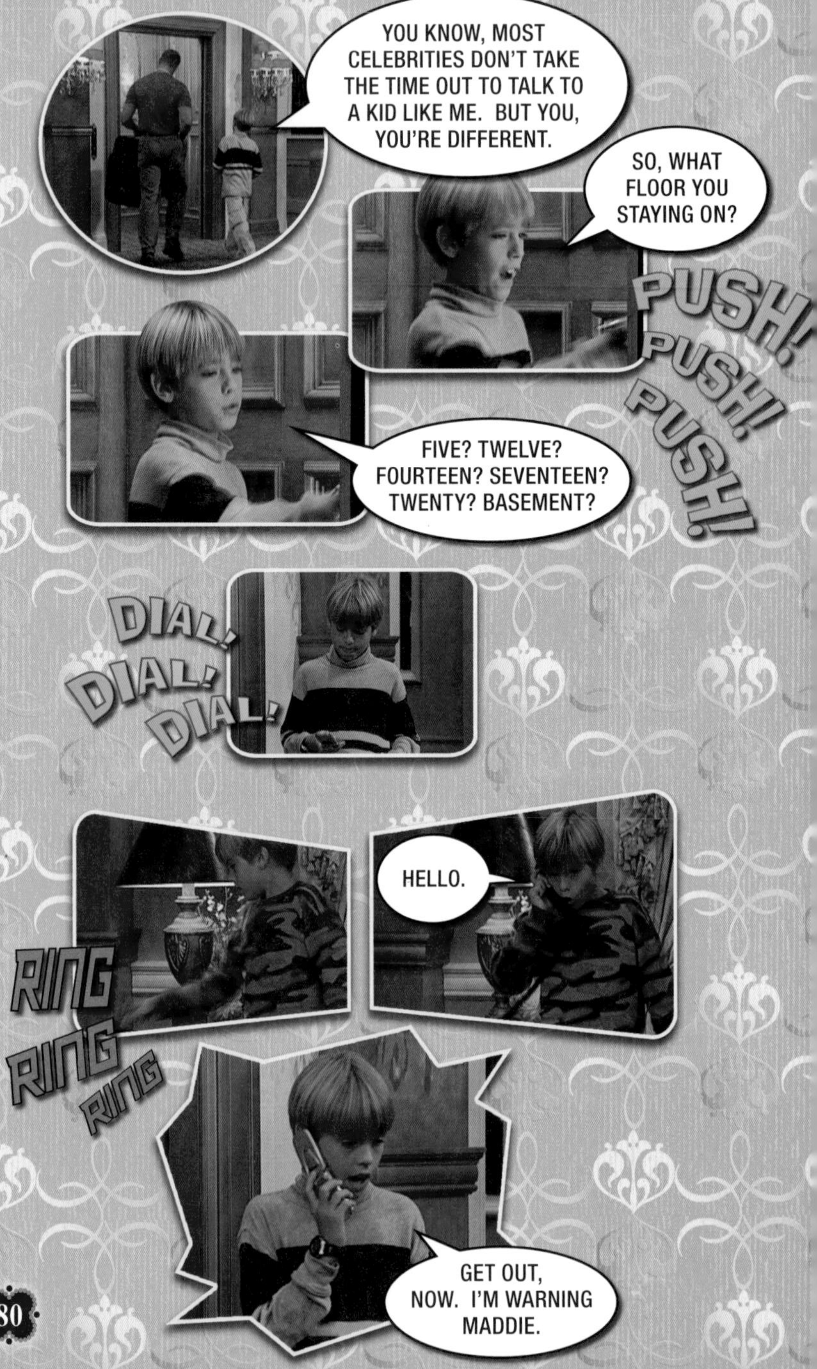
YOU KNOW, MOST CELEBRITIES DON'T TAKE THE TIME OUT TO TALK TO A KID LIKE ME. BUT YOU, YOU'RE DIFFERENT.
SO, WHAT FLOOR YOU STAYING ON?
PUSH! PUSH! PUSH!
FIVE? TWELVE? FOURTEEN? SEVENTEEN? TWENTY? BASEMENT?
DIAL! DIAL! DIAL!
RING RING RING
HELLO.
GET OUT, NOW. I'M WARNING MADDIE.

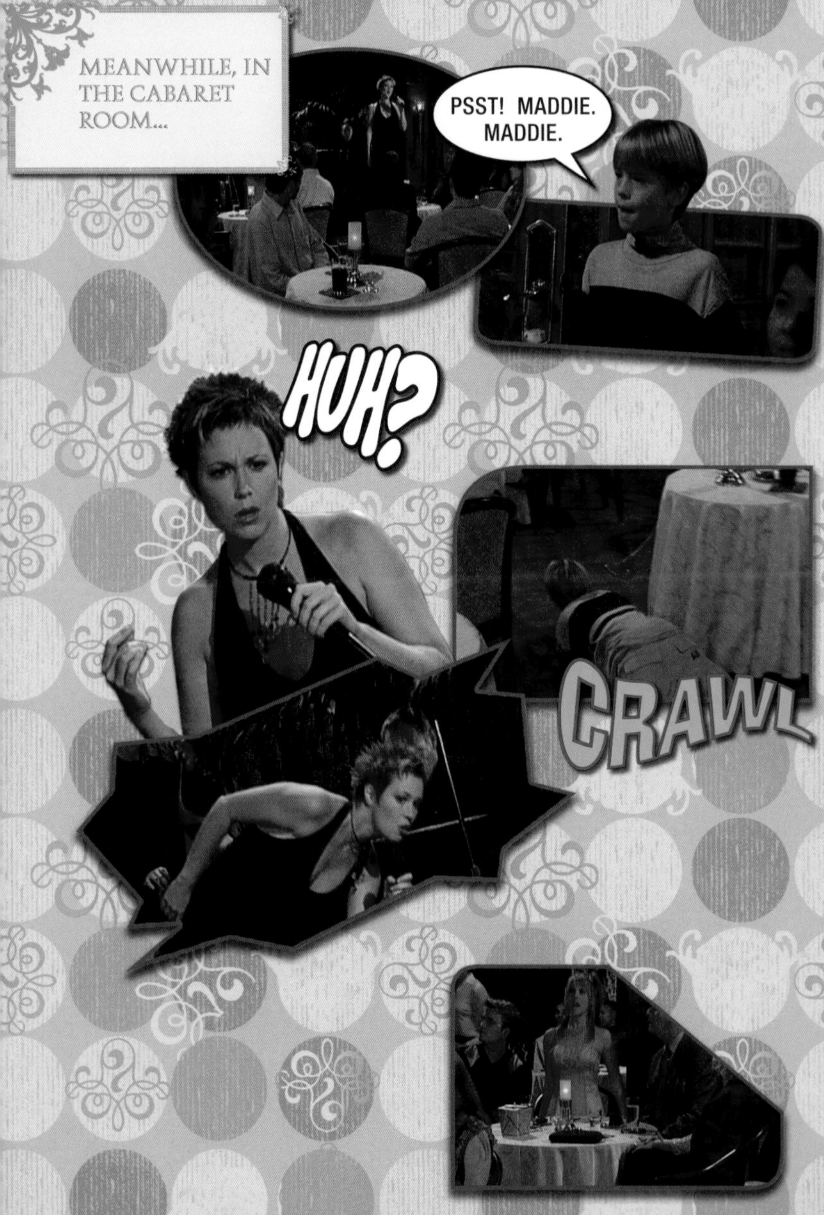
MEANWHILE, IN THE CABARET ROOM...
PSST! MADDIE. MADDIE.
HUH?
CRAWL

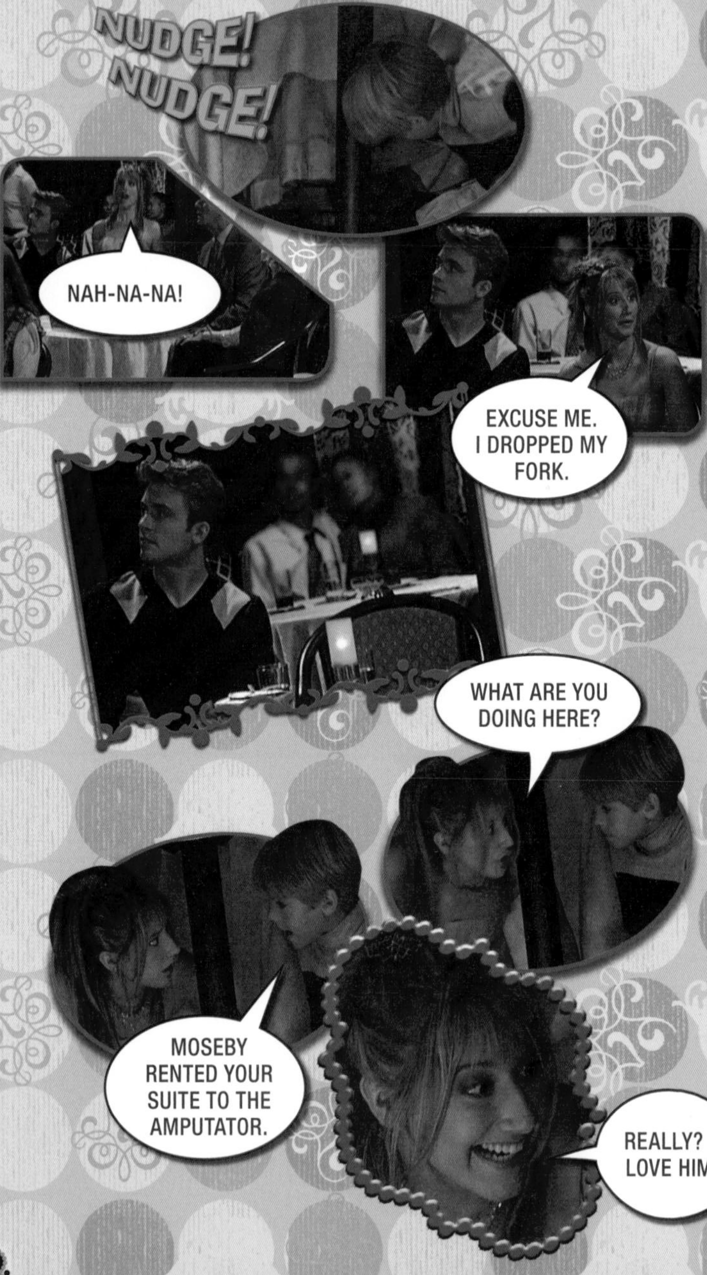
NUDGE! NUDGE!
NAH-NA-NA!
EXCUSE ME. I DROPPED MY FORK.
WHAT ARE YOU DOING HERE?
MOSEBY RENTED YOUR SUITE TO THE AMPUTATOR.
REALLY? I LOVE HIM.

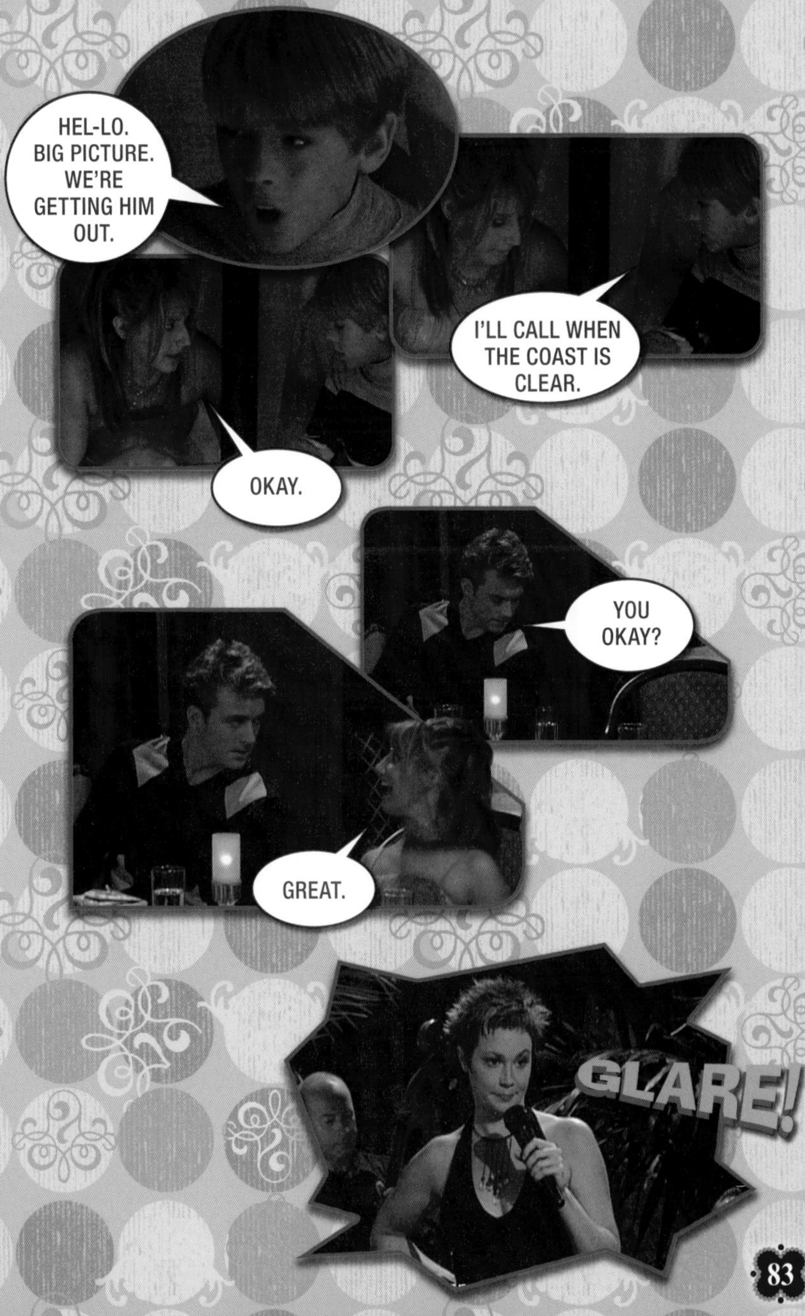
HEL-LO. BIG PICTURE. WE'RE GETTING HIM OUT.
I'LL CALL WHEN THE COAST IS CLEAR.
OKAY.
YOU OKAY?
GREAT.
GLARE!

IN THE IMPERIAL SUITE...

QUICK!

DROP!

DASH!

OOO, A QUARTER.

BEND

ZACK CLOSES THE DOOR BEFORE AMPUTATOR SEES HIM...

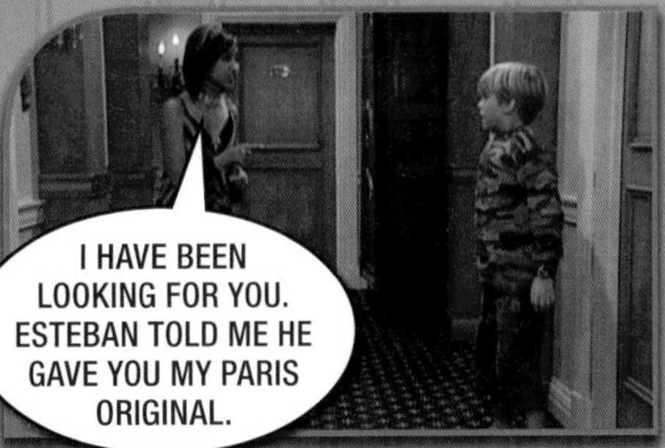
I HAVE BEEN LOOKING FOR YOU. ESTEBAN TOLD ME HE GAVE YOU MY PARIS ORIGINAL.

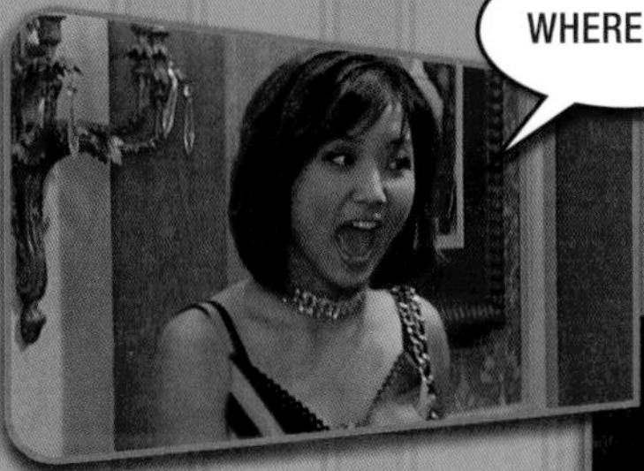
WHERE IS IT?

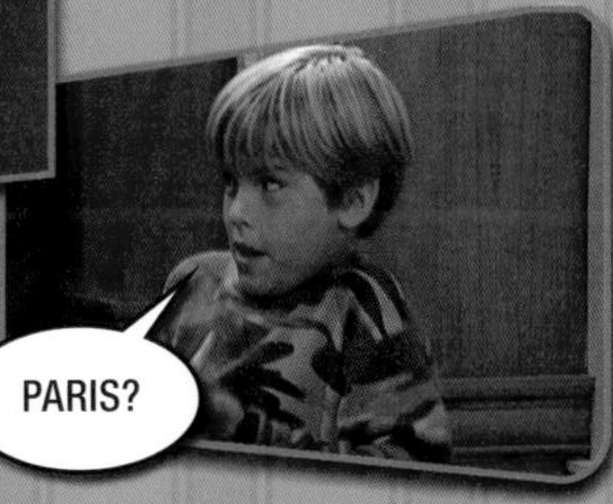
PARIS?

MEANWHILE, INSIDE THE SUITE, AMPUTATOR PUTS HIS BAG ON THE TABLE AND IT COLLAPSES.

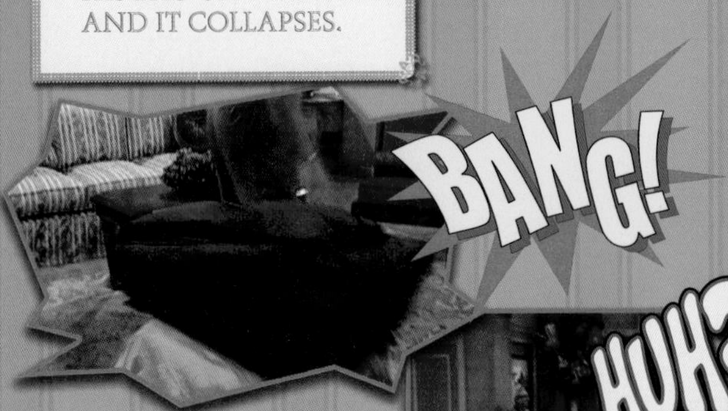
BANG!

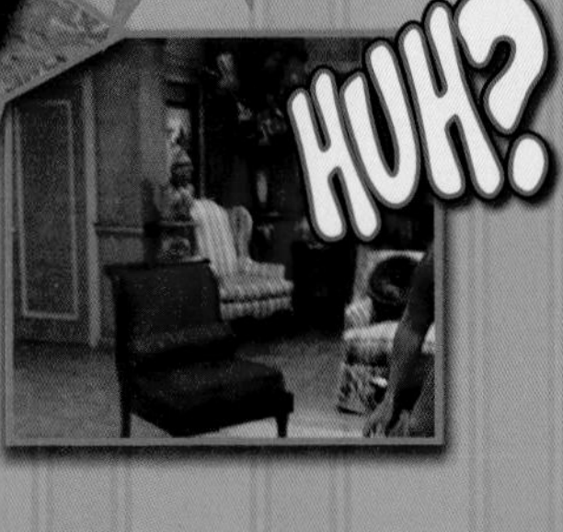
HUH?

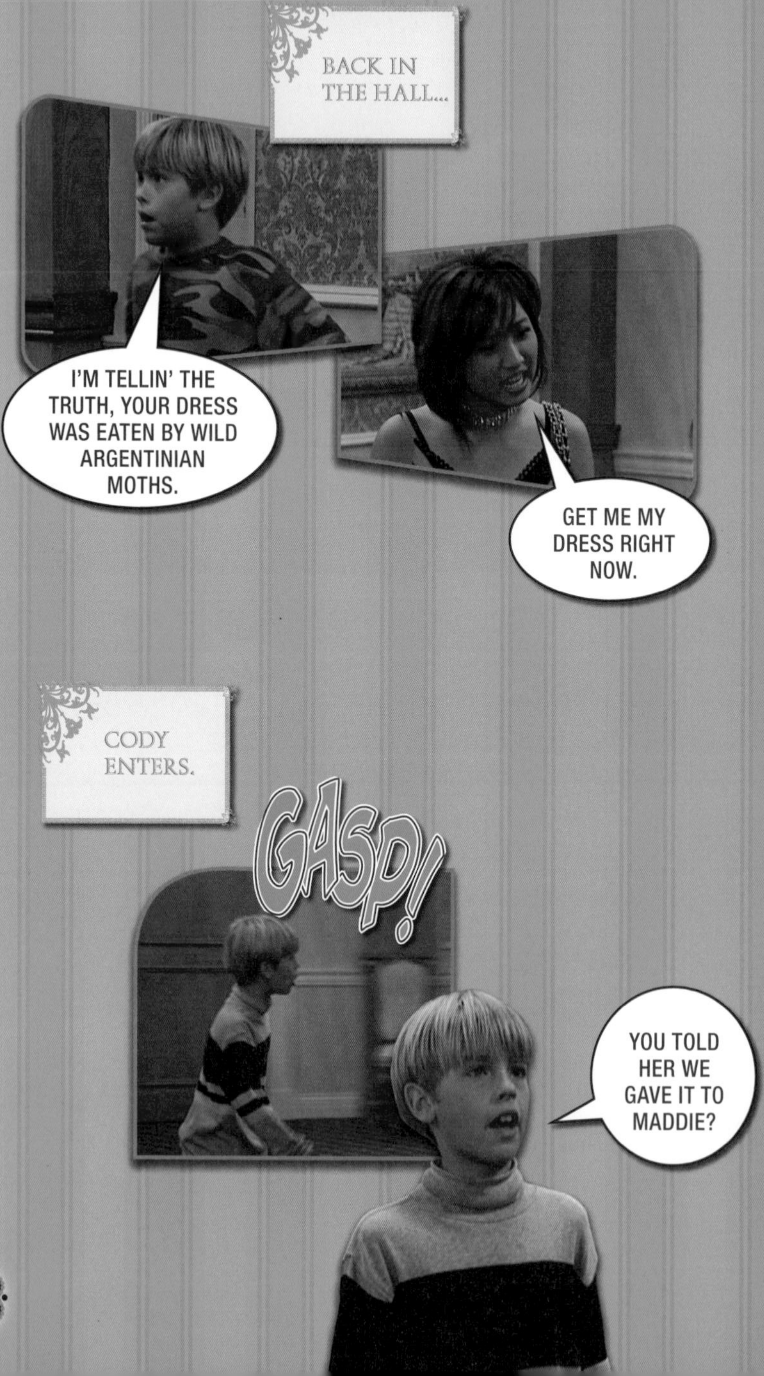
BACK IN THE HALL...
I'M TELLIN' THE TRUTH, YOUR DRESS WAS EATEN BY WILD ARGENTINIAN MOTHS.
GET ME MY DRESS RIGHT NOW.
CODY ENTERS.
GASP!
YOU TOLD HER WE GAVE IT TO MADDIE?

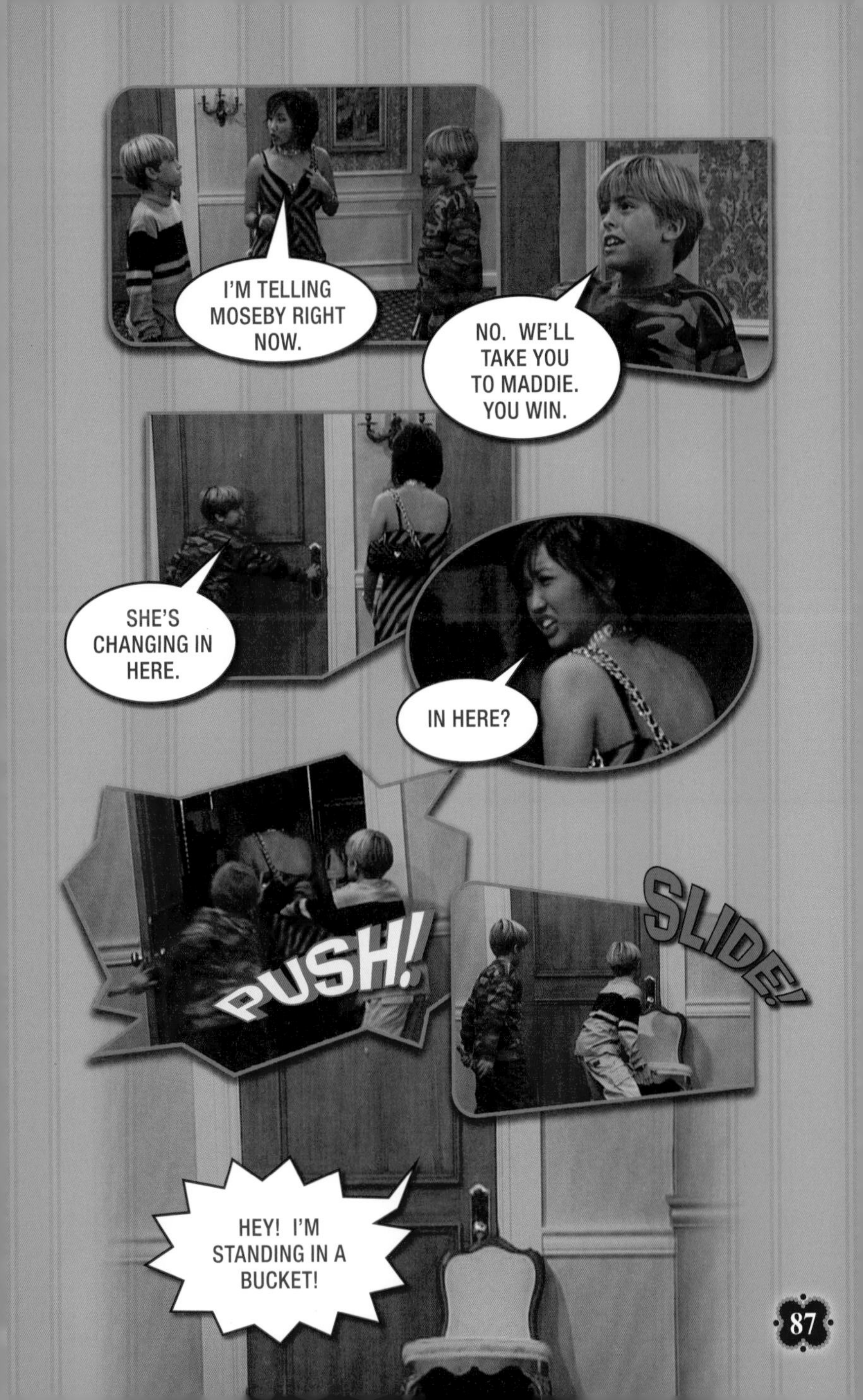
I'M TELLING MOSEBY RIGHT NOW.
NO. WE'LL TAKE YOU TO MADDIE. YOU WIN.
SHE'S CHANGING IN HERE.
IN HERE?
PUSH!
SLIDE!
HEY! I'M STANDING IN A BUCKET!

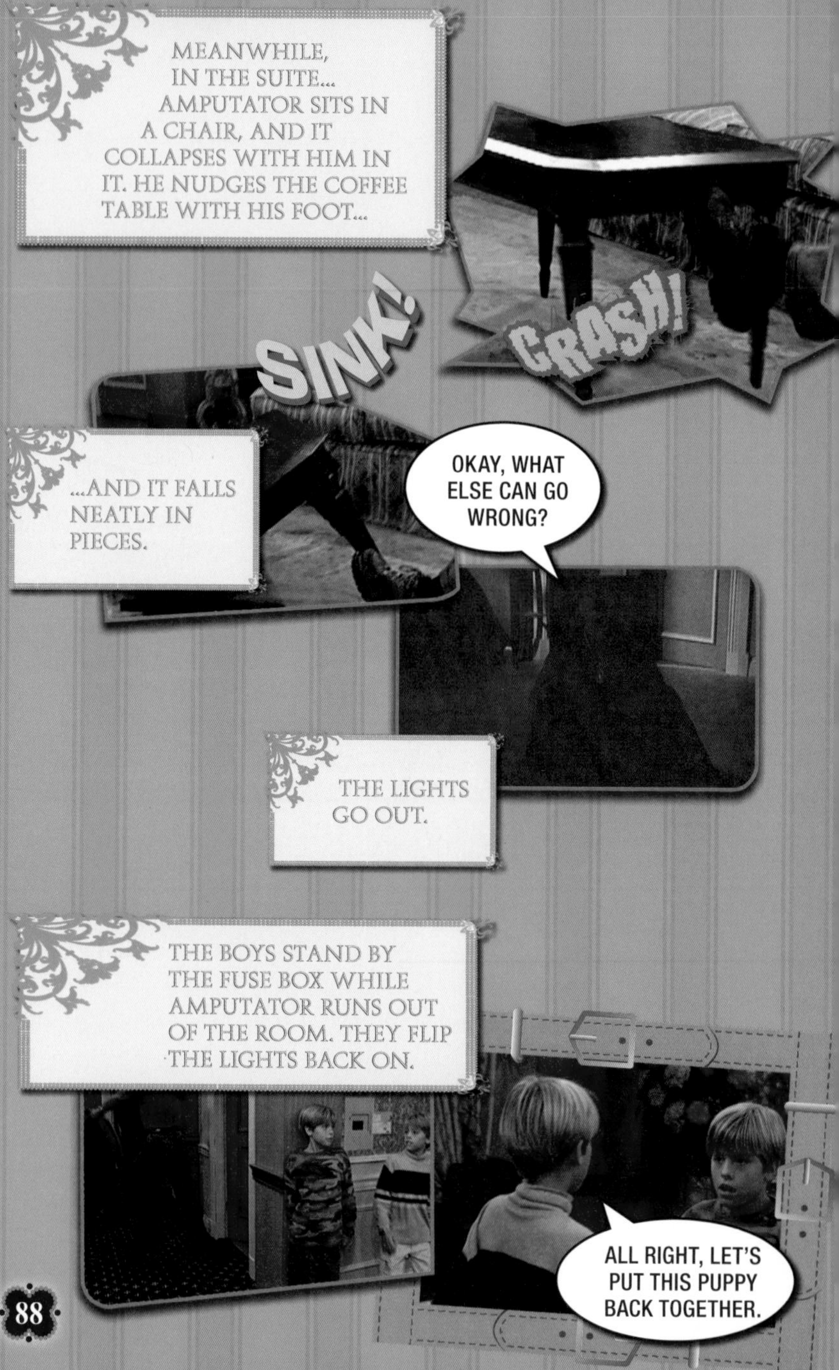
MEANWHILE, IN THE SUITE... AMPUTATOR SITS IN A CHAIR, AND IT COLLAPSES WITH HIM IN IT. HE NUDGES THE COFFEE TABLE WITH HIS FOOT...
CRASH!
SINK!
...AND IT FALLS NEATLY IN PIECES.
OKAY, WHAT ELSE CAN GO WRONG?
THE LIGHTS GO OUT.
THE BOYS STAND BY THE FUSE BOX WHILE AMPUTATOR RUNS OUT OF THE ROOM. THEY FLIP THE LIGHTS BACK ON.
ALL RIGHT, LET'S PUT THIS PUPPY BACK TOGETHER.

BACK IN THE CABARET ROOM, A SHORT TIME LATER, JASON'S MOM TELLS CAREY ABOUT MADDIE'S NEW SUITE...

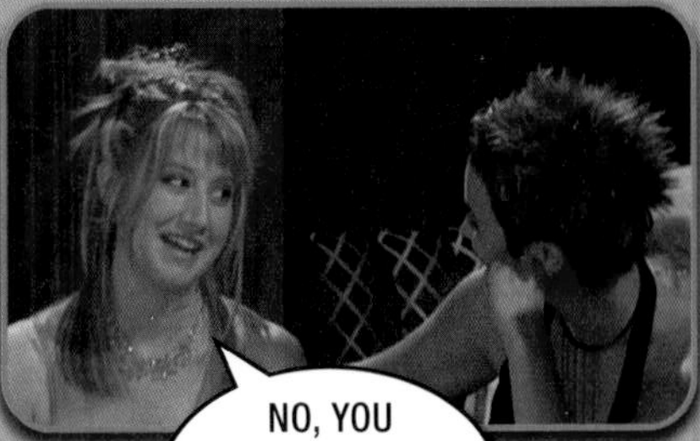
NO, YOU DON'T WANT TO SEE MY NEW SUITE.

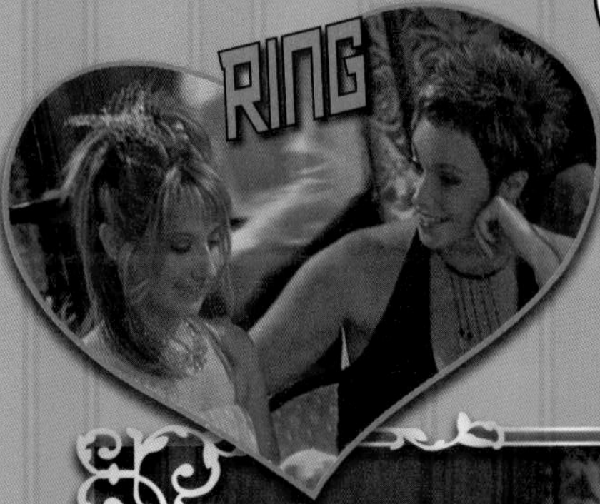
RING

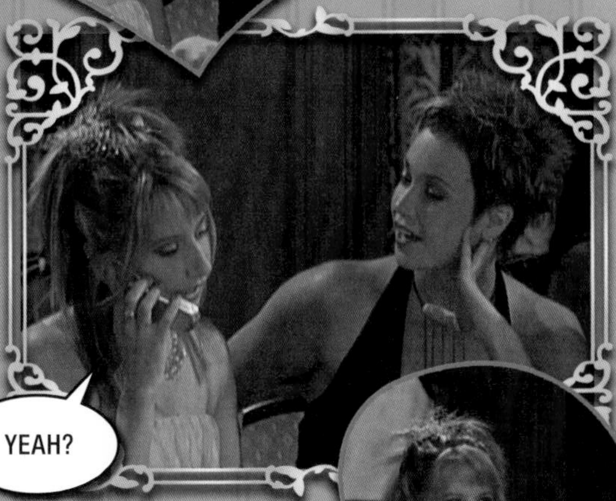
YEAH?

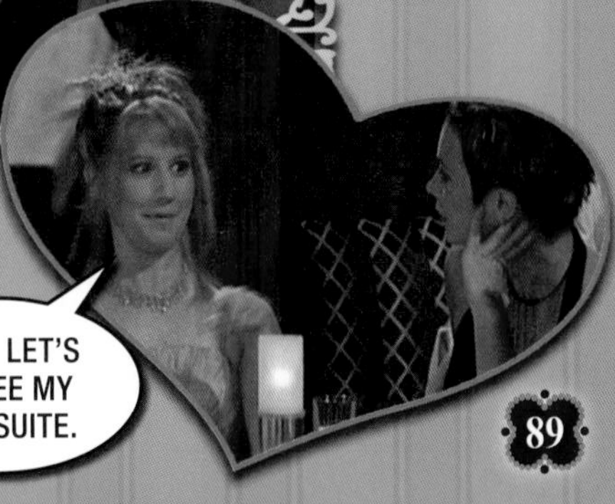
OKAY, LET'S GO SEE MY NEW SUITE.

A SHORT TIME LATER...

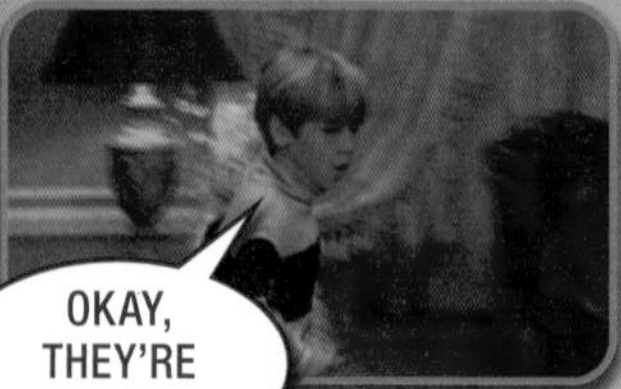
OKAY, THEY'RE COMING.

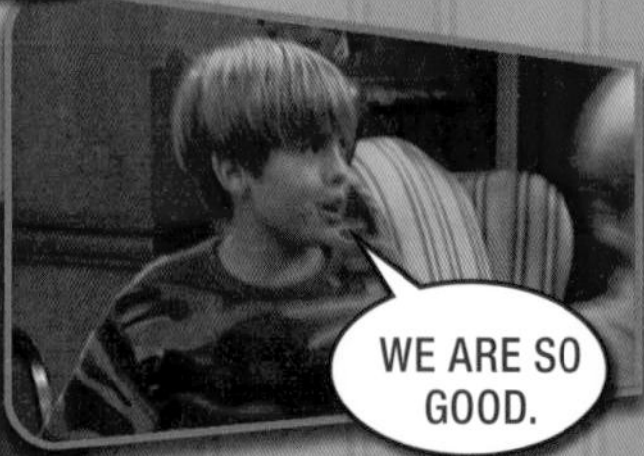
WE ARE SO GOOD.

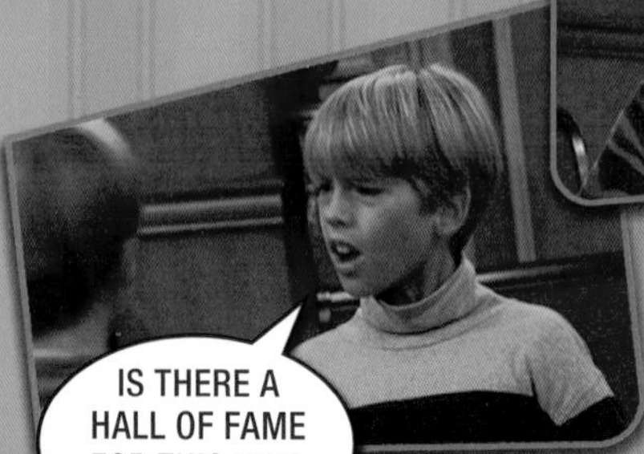
IS THERE A HALL OF FAME FOR THIS KIND OF STUFF?

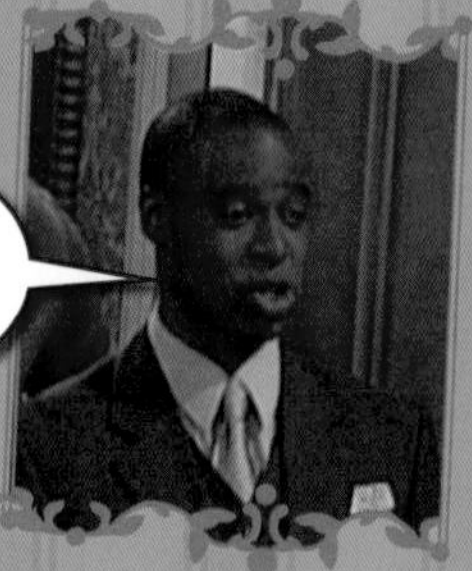
YES, IT'S CALLED PRISON.

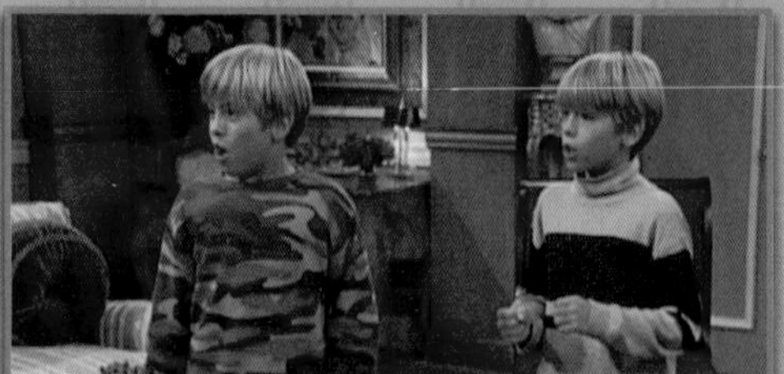
MR. MOSEBY!

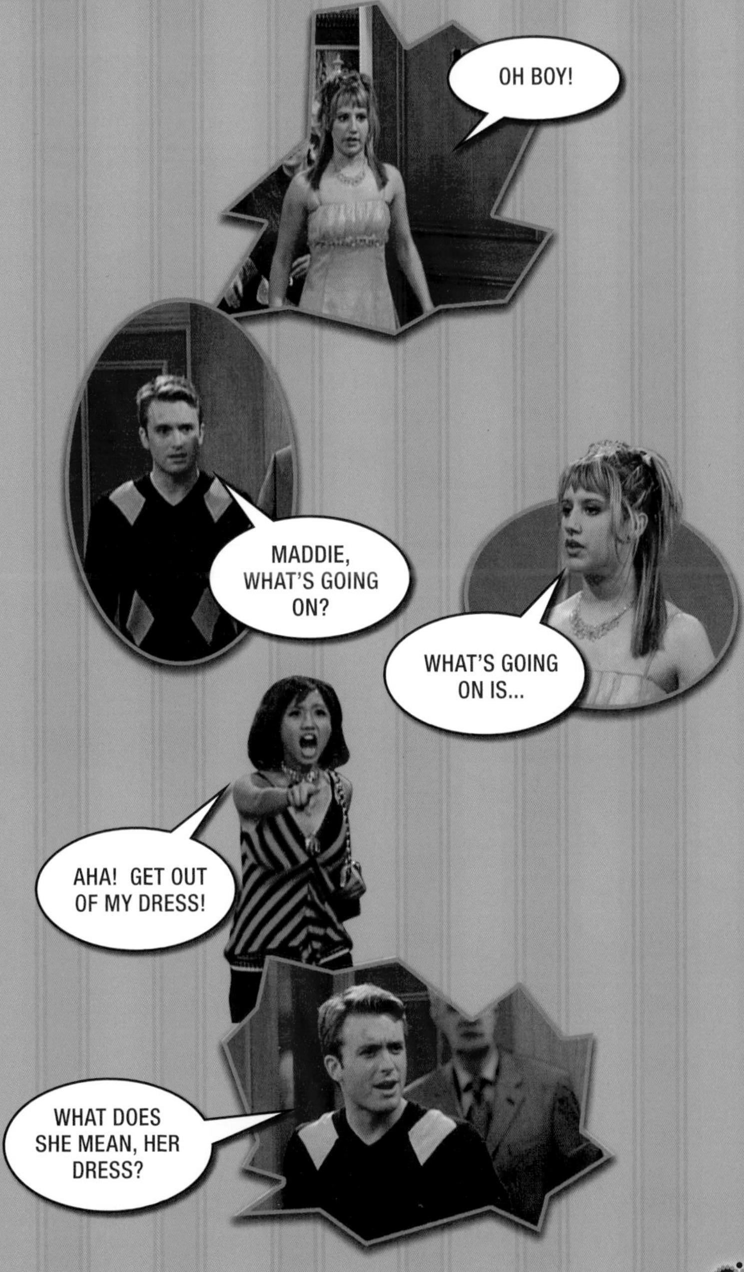
OH BOY!
MADDIE, WHAT'S GOING ON?
WHAT'S GOING ON IS...
AHA! GET OUT OF MY DRESS!
WHAT DOES SHE MEAN, HER DRESS?

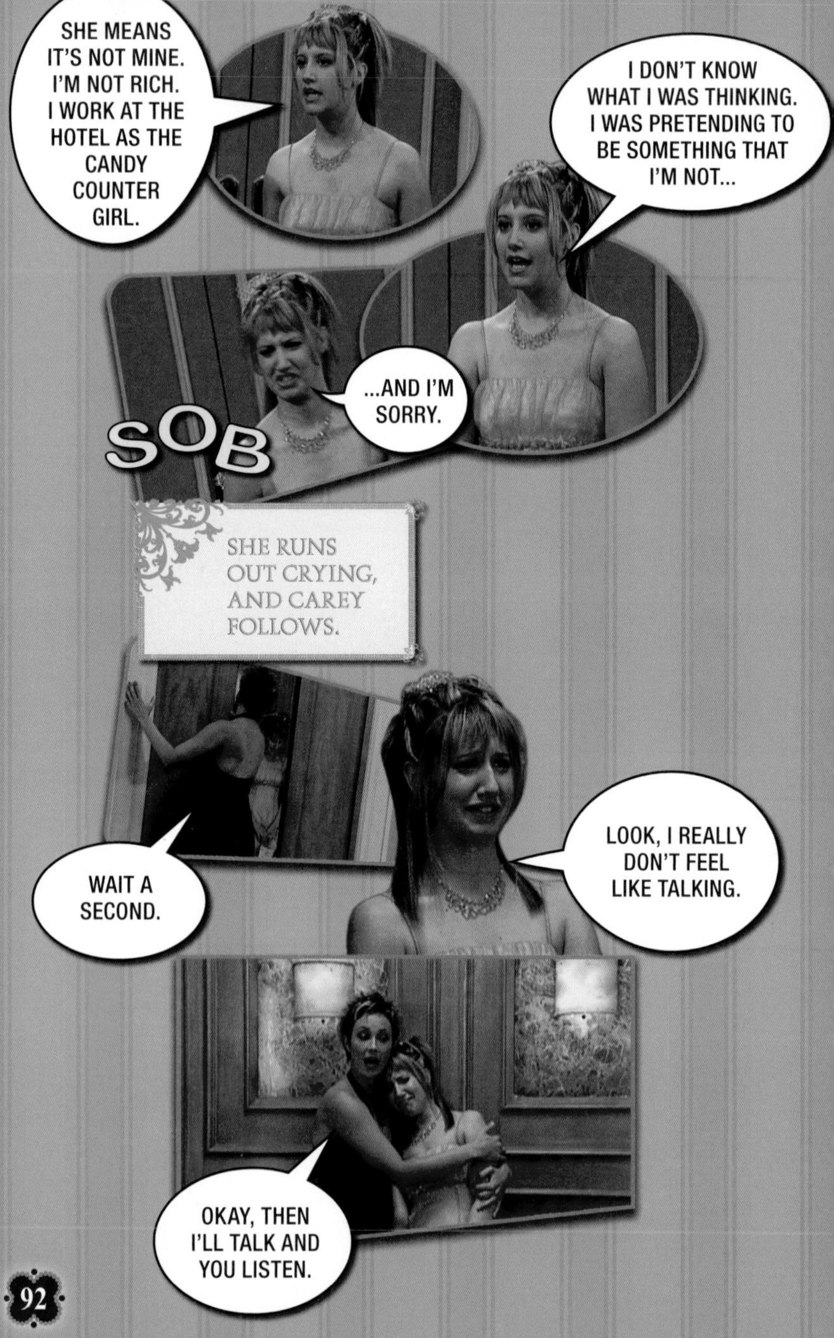
SHE MEANS IT'S NOT MINE. I'M NOT RICH. I WORK AT THE HOTEL AS THE CANDY COUNTER GIRL.
I DON'T KNOW WHAT I WAS THINKING. I WAS PRETENDING TO BE SOMETHING THAT I'M NOT...
...AND I'M SORRY.
SOB
SHE RUNS OUT CRYING, AND CAREY FOLLOWS.
WAIT A SECOND.
LOOK, I REALLY DON'T FEEL LIKE TALKING.
OKAY, THEN I'LL TALK AND YOU LISTEN.

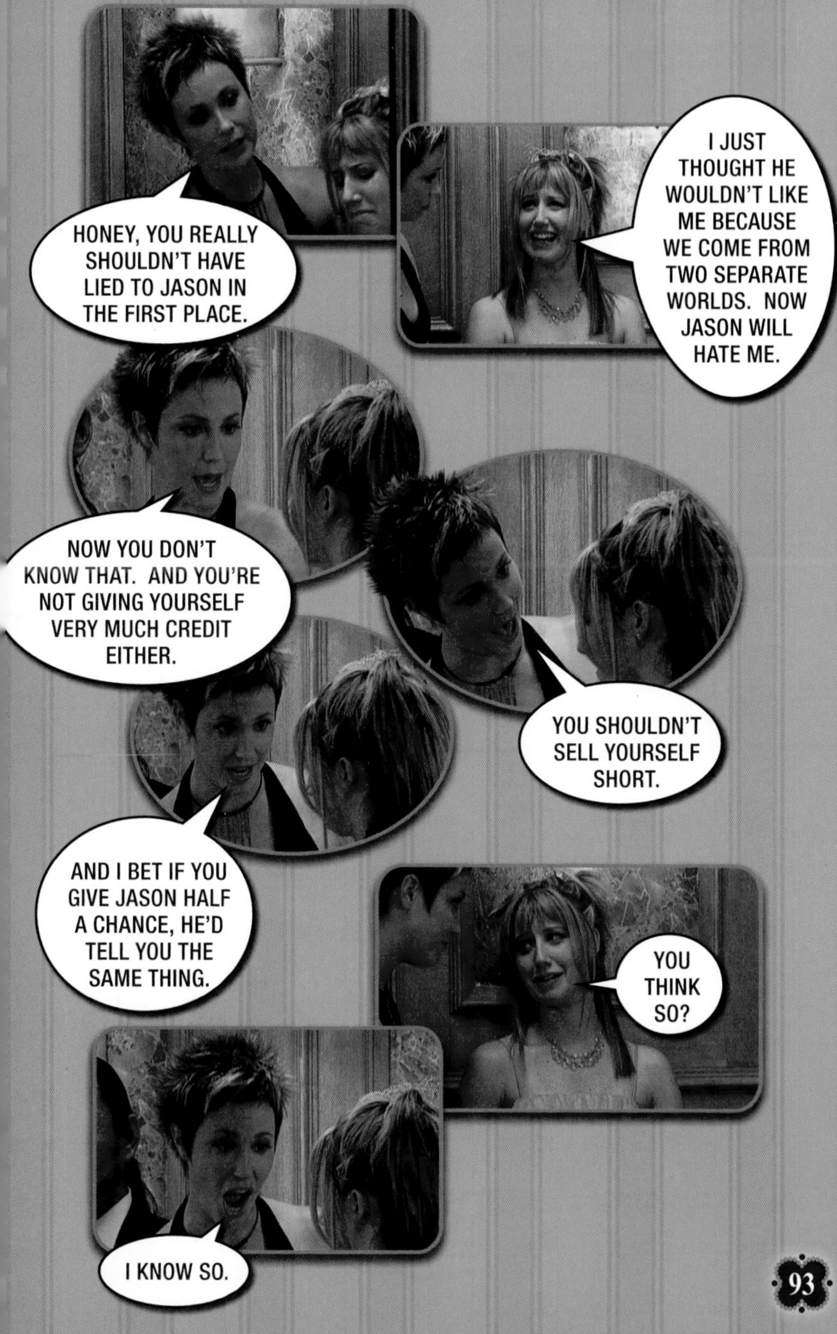
HONEY, YOU REALLY SHOULDN'T HAVE LIED TO JASON IN THE FIRST PLACE.
I JUST THOUGHT HE WOULDN'T LIKE ME BECAUSE WE COME FROM TWO SEPARATE WORLDS. NOW JASON WILL HATE ME.
NOW YOU DON'T KNOW THAT. AND YOU'RE NOT GIVING YOURSELF VERY MUCH CREDIT EITHER.
YOU SHOULDN'T SELL YOURSELF SHORT.
AND I BET IF YOU GIVE JASON HALF A CHANCE, HE'D TELL YOU THE SAME THING.
YOU THINK SO?
I KNOW SO.

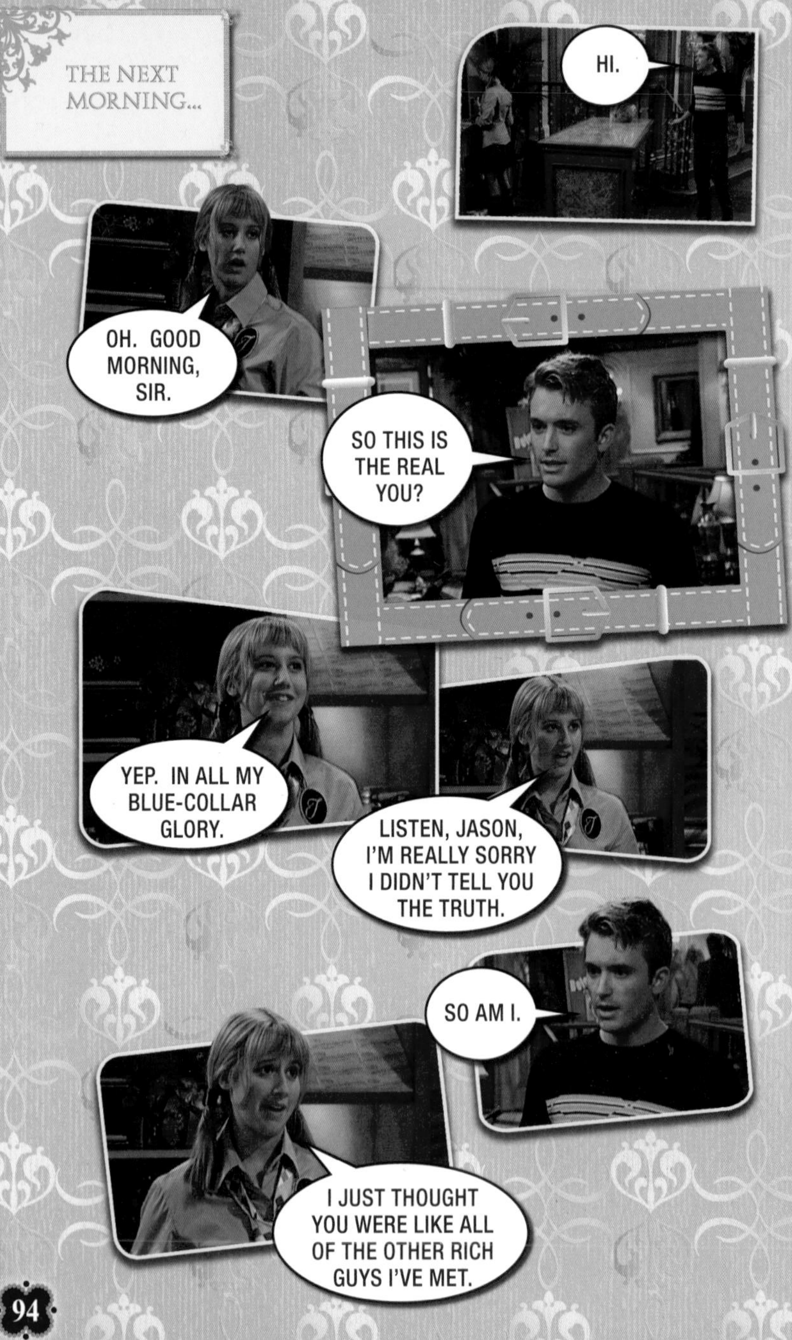
THE NEXT MORNING...
HI.
OH. GOOD MORNING, SIR.
SO THIS IS THE REAL YOU?
YEP. IN ALL MY BLUE-COLLAR GLORY.
LISTEN, JASON, I'M REALLY SORRY I DIDN'T TELL YOU THE TRUTH.
SO AM I.
I JUST THOUGHT YOU WERE LIKE ALL OF THE OTHER RICH GUYS I'VE MET.

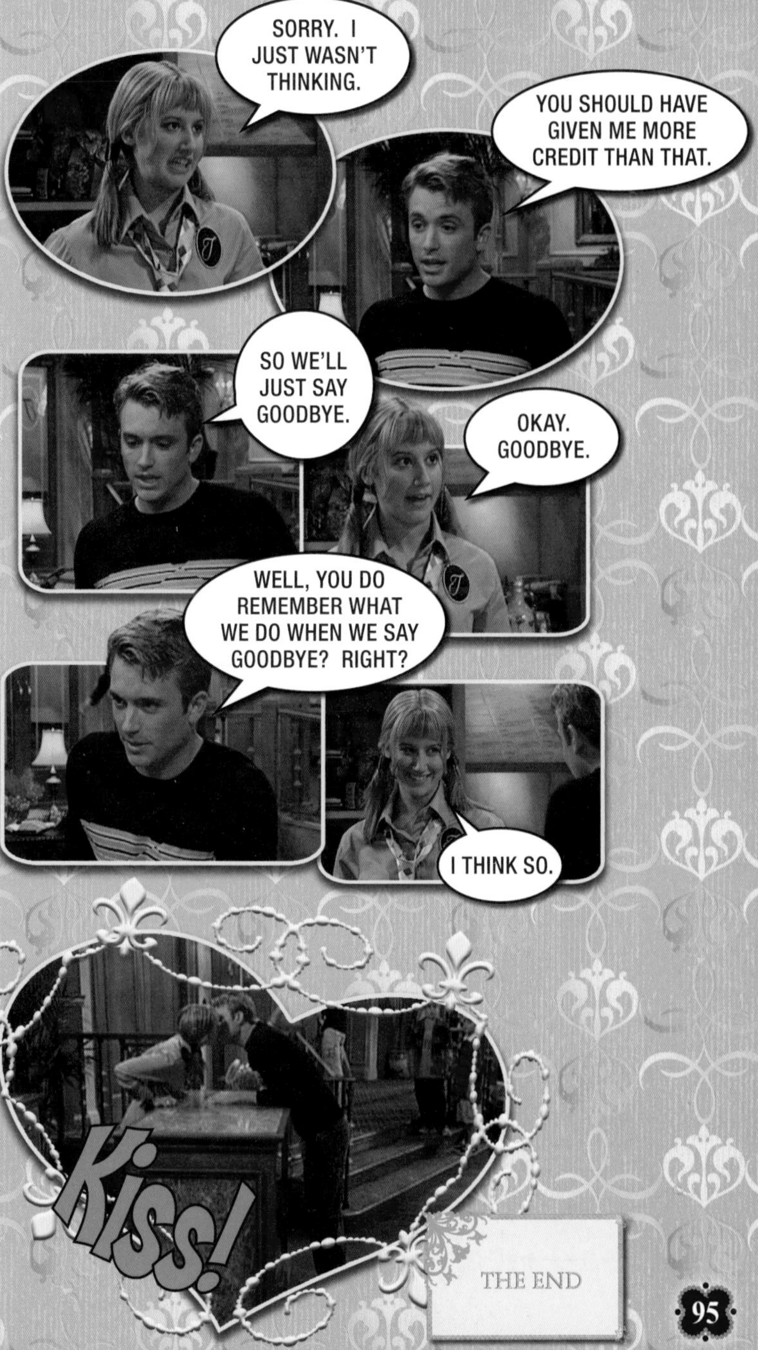
SORRY. I JUST WASN'T THINKING.
YOU SHOULD HAVE GIVEN ME MORE CREDIT THAN THAT.
SO WE'LL JUST SAY GOODBYE.
OKAY. GOODBYE.
WELL, YOU DO REMEMBER WHAT WE DO WHEN WE SAY GOODBYE? RIGHT?
I THINK SO.
Kiss!
THE END

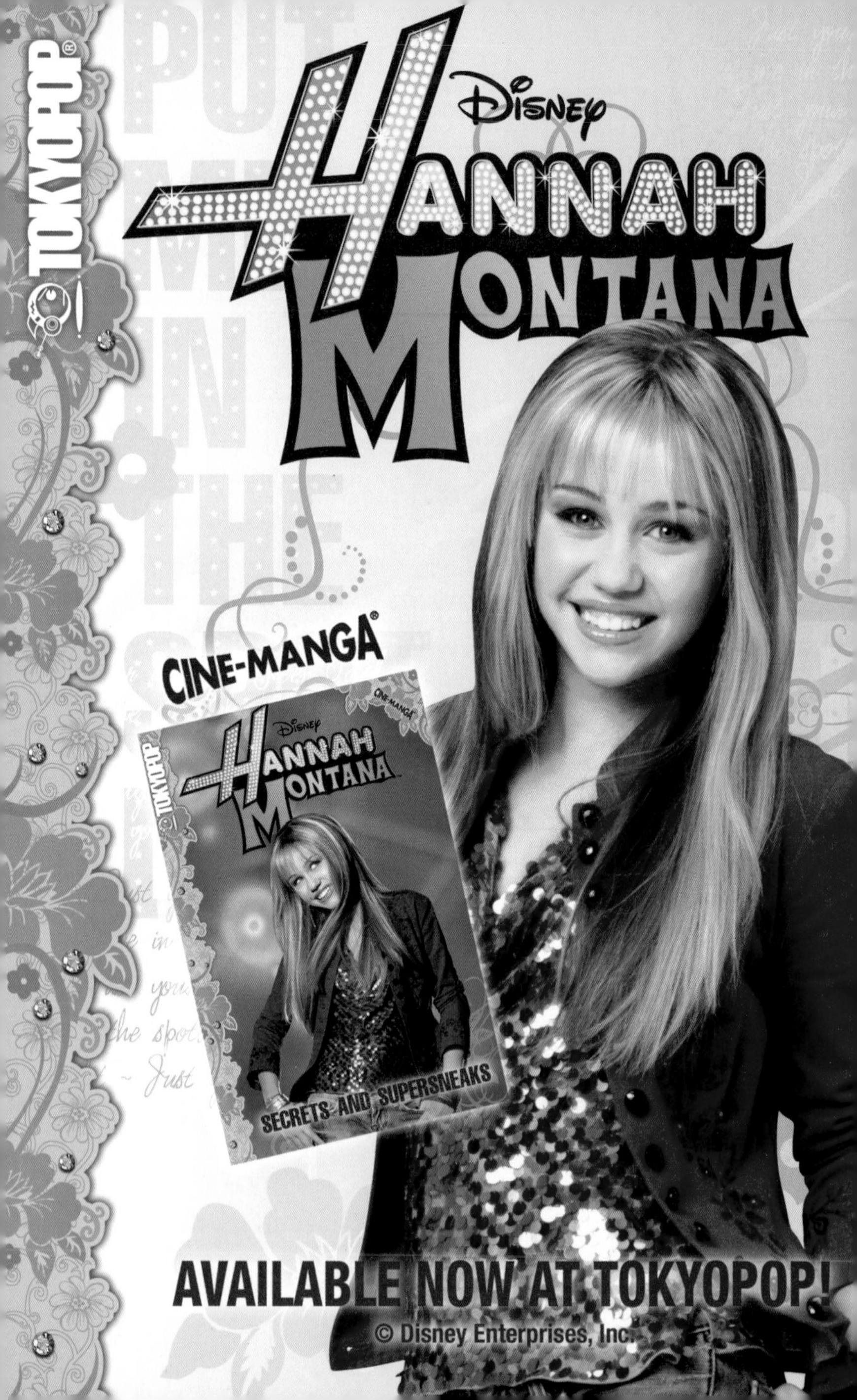
TOKYOPOP
DISNEY
HANNAH MONTANA
CINE-MANGA
DISNEY
HANNAH MONTANA
CINE-MANGA
TOKYOPOP
SECRETS AND SUPERSNEAKS
AVAILABLE NOW AT TOKYOPOP!
© Disney Enterprises, Inc.